USE THIS PAGE TO TEST YOUR COLORING TOOLS

The Coloring Book of Stamps
Famous Americans

The Cross Little Institute of Relaxation Therapy

Copyright © 2018 The Cross Little Company

All rights reserved.

ISBN: 9781729300442
Imprint: Independently published

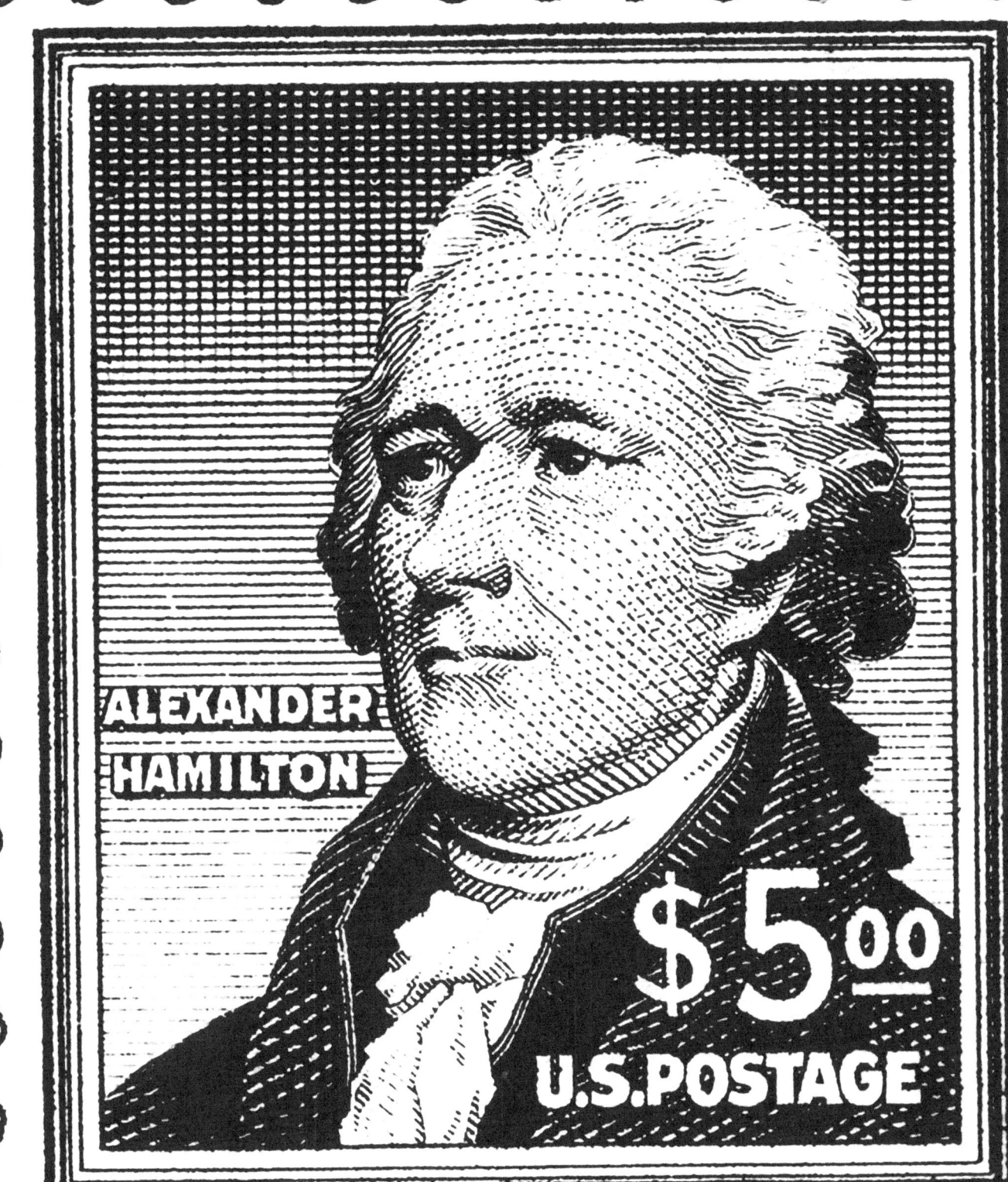

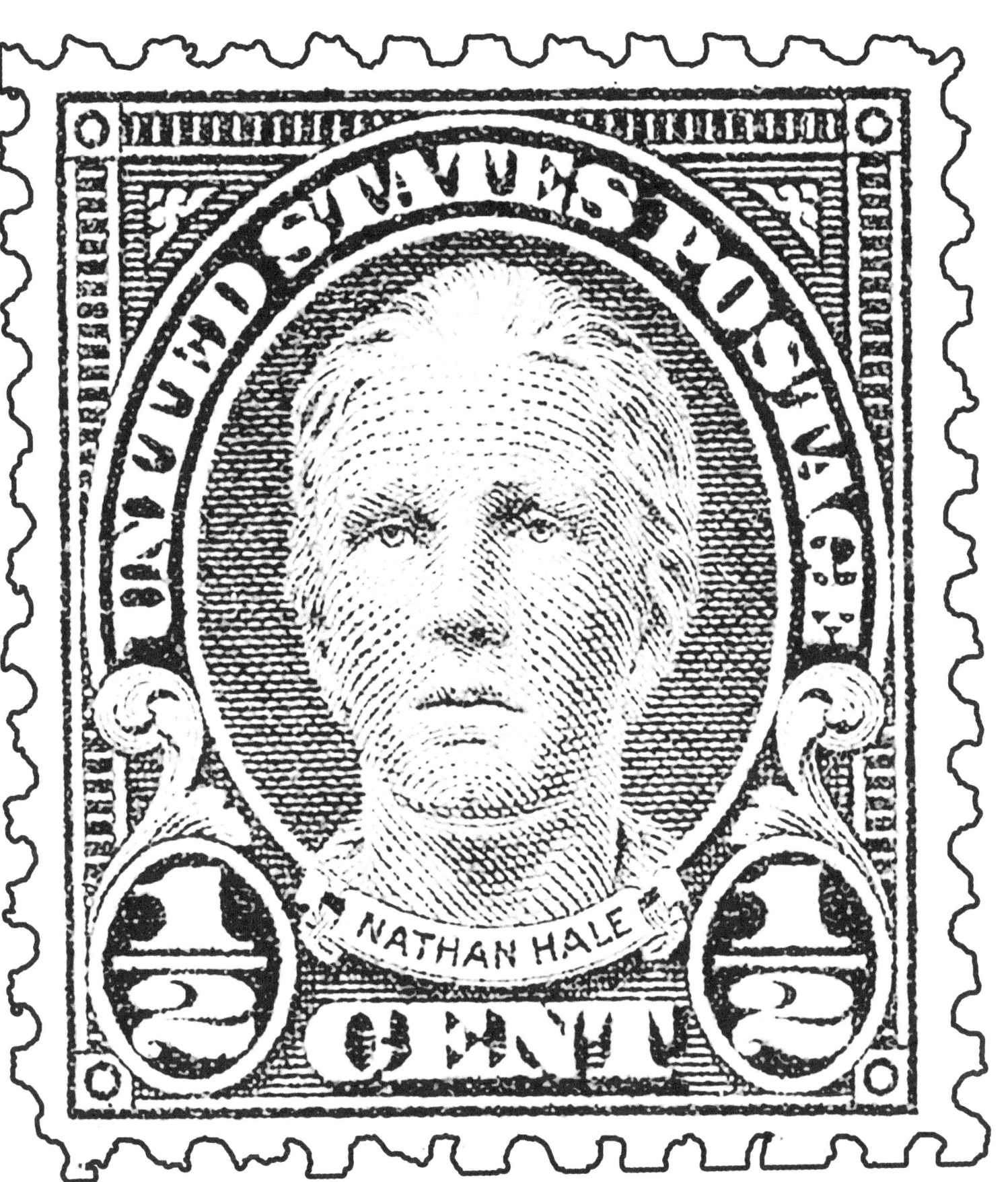

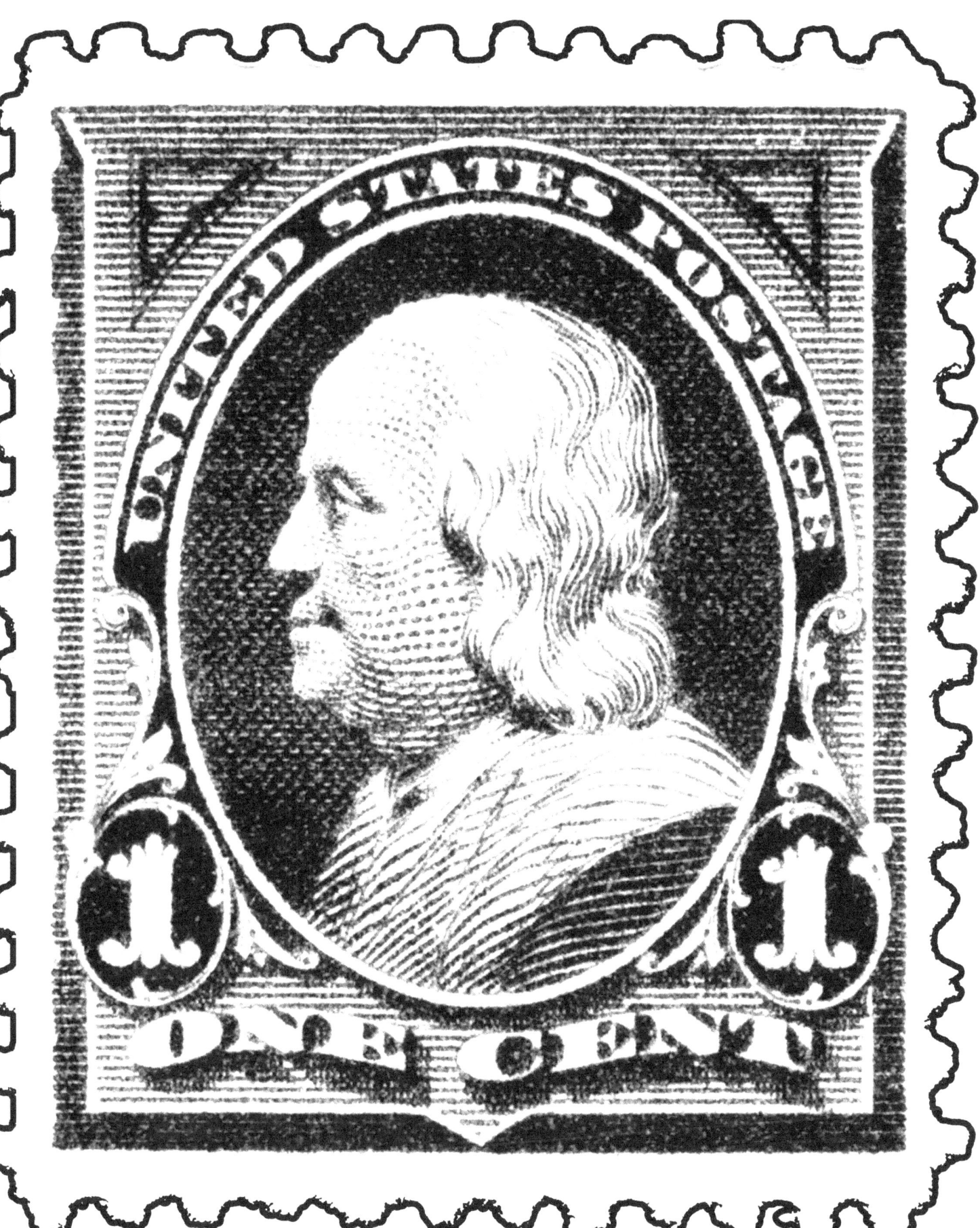

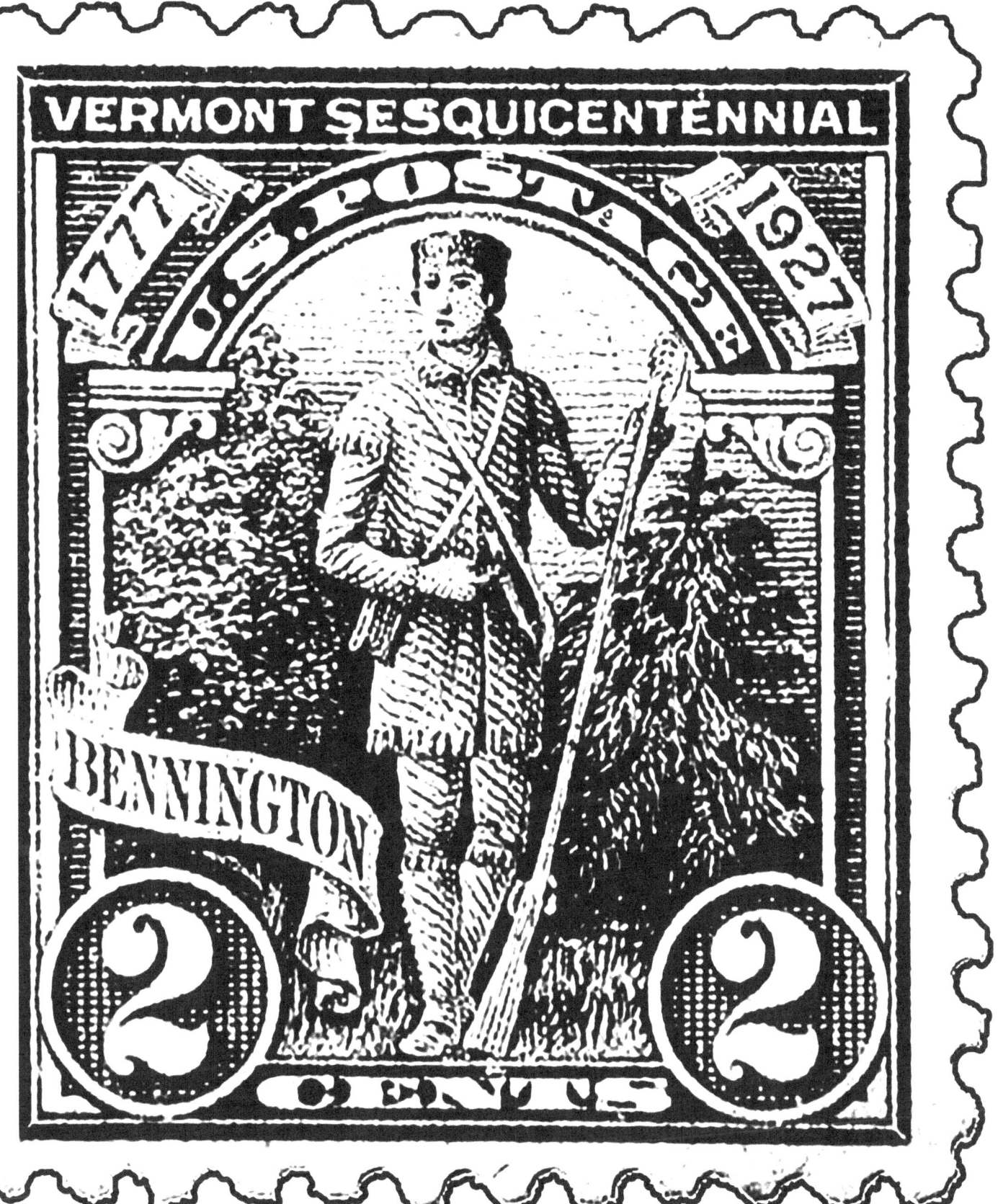

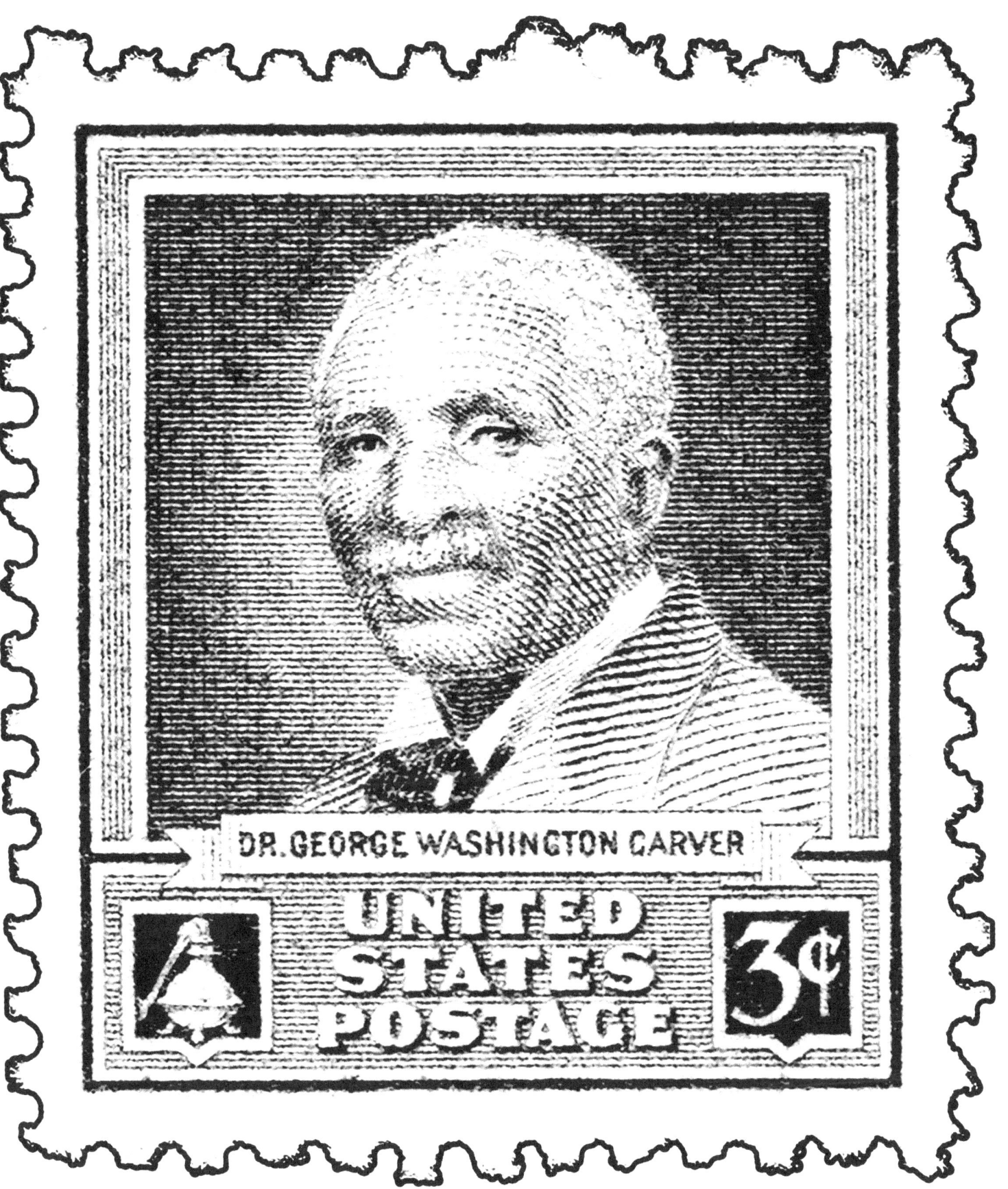

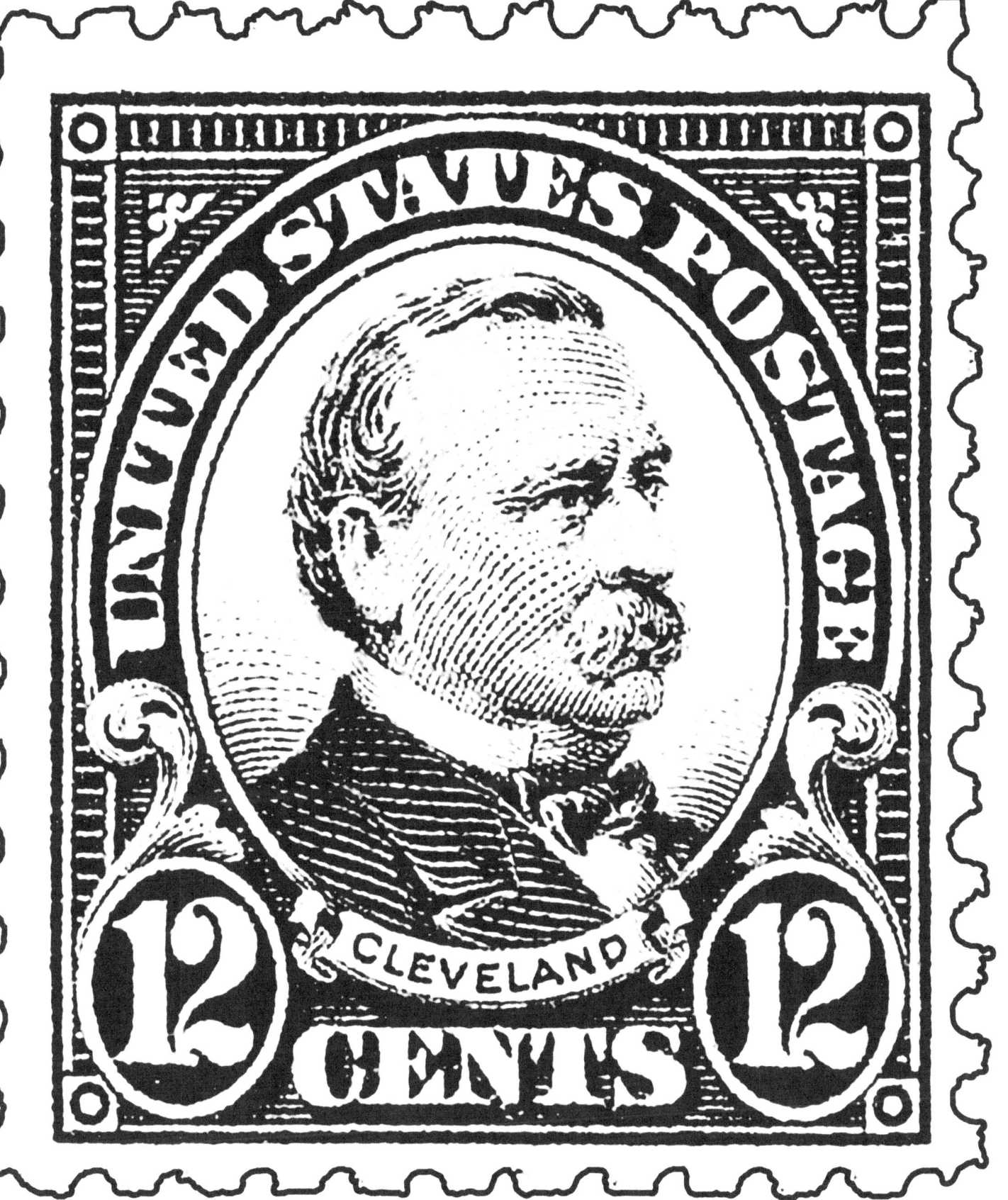

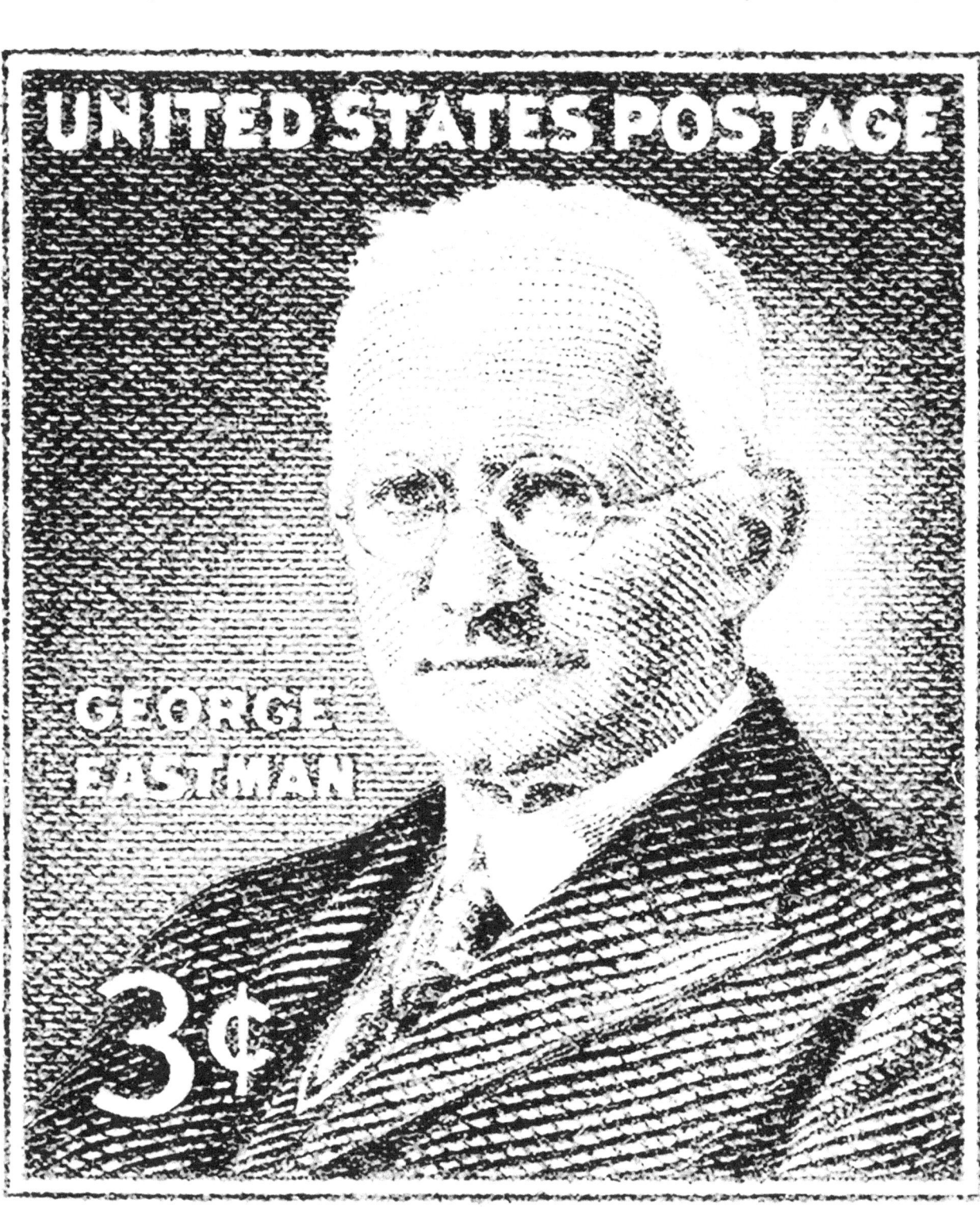

UNITED STATES POSTAGE

THOMAS A. EDISON

3¢

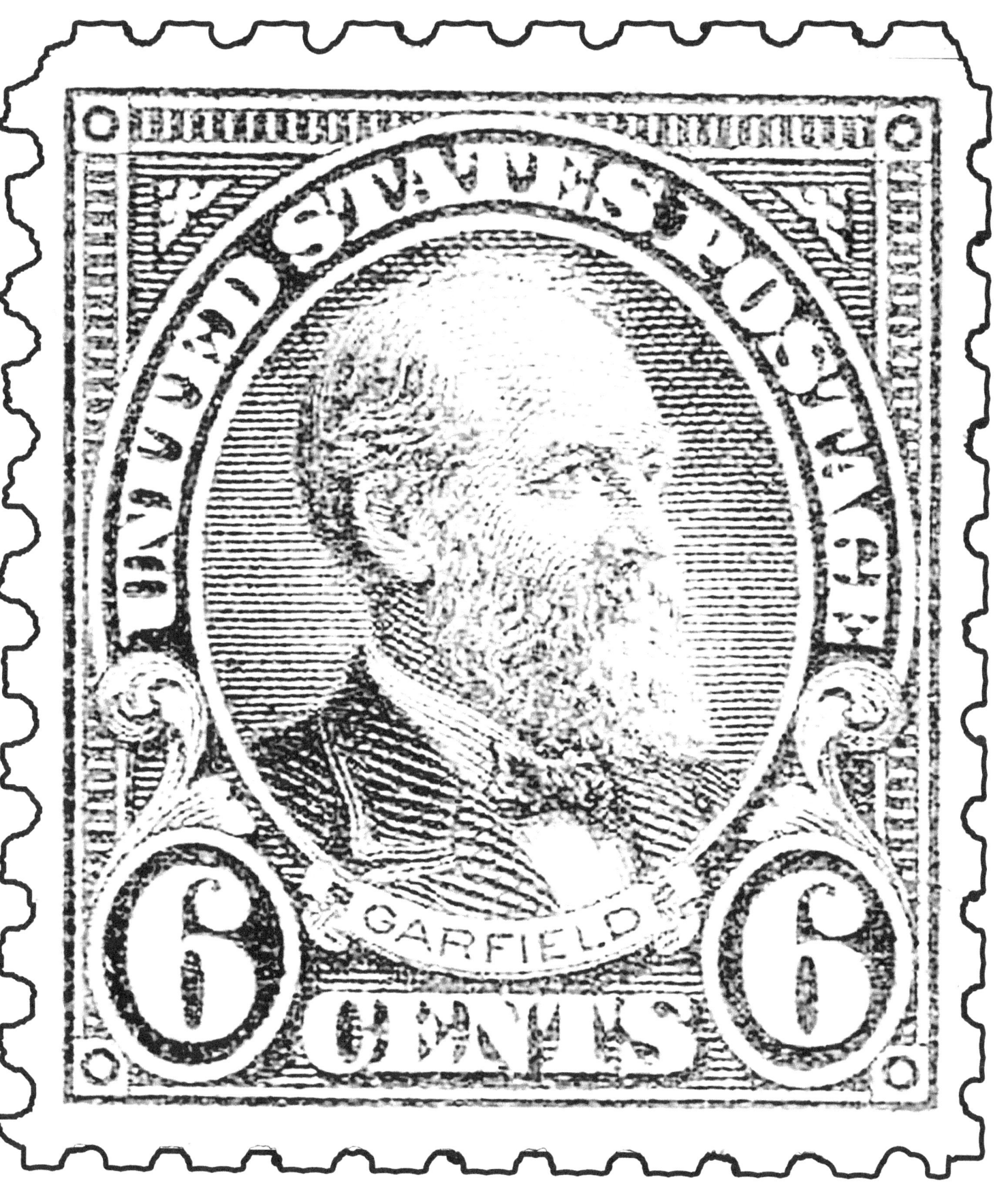

UNITED STATES POSTAGE

SAMUEL GOMPERS

3¢

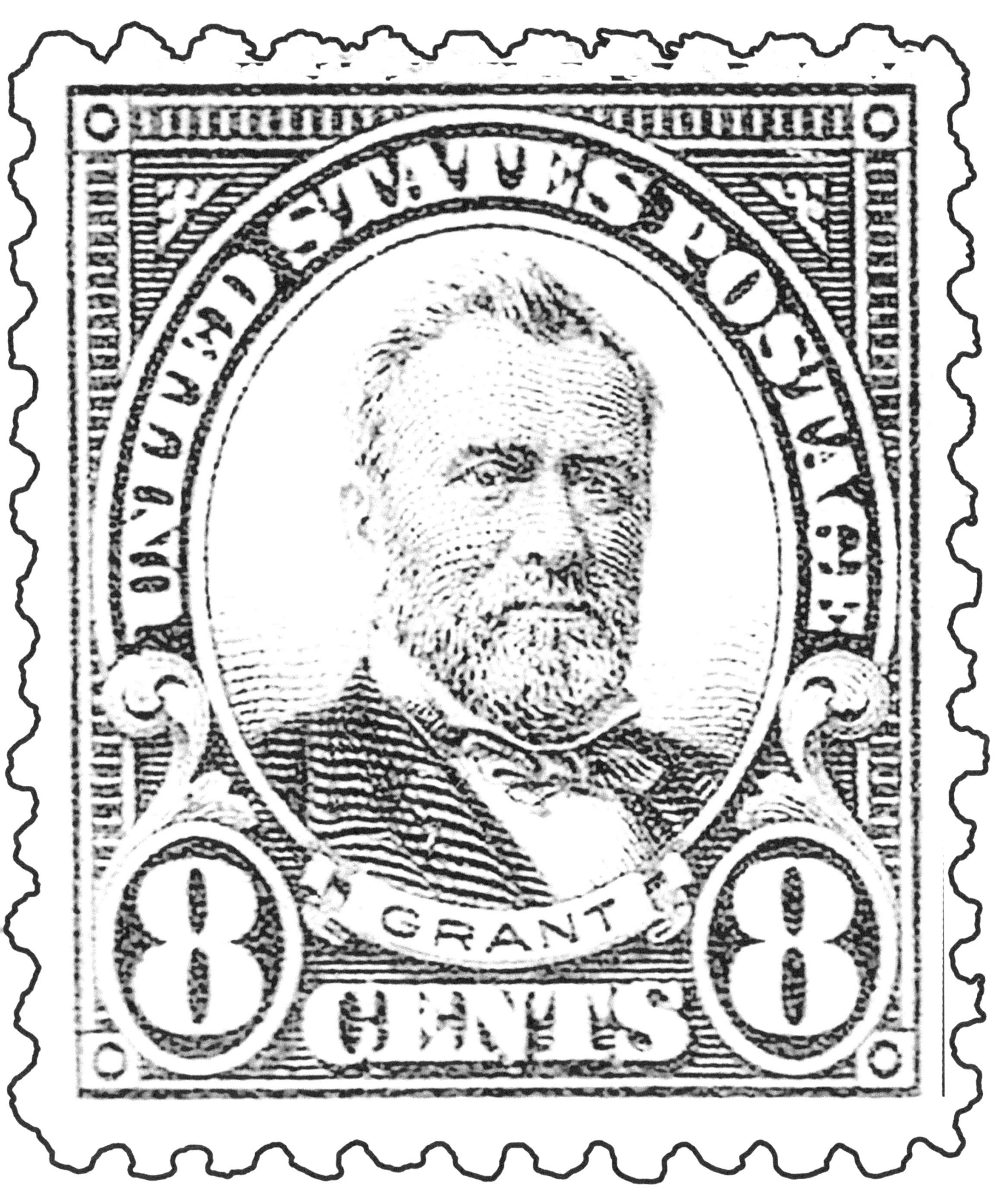

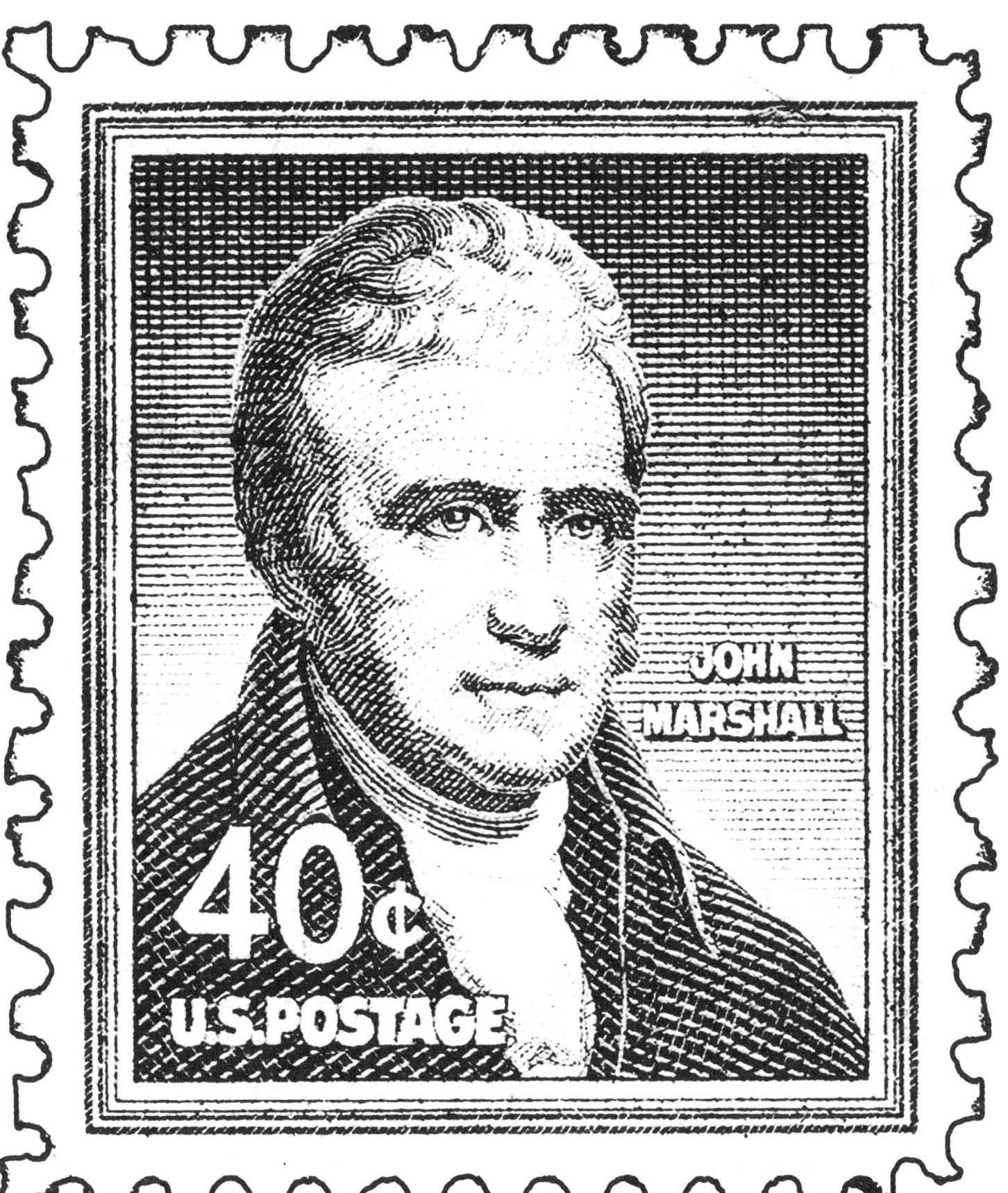

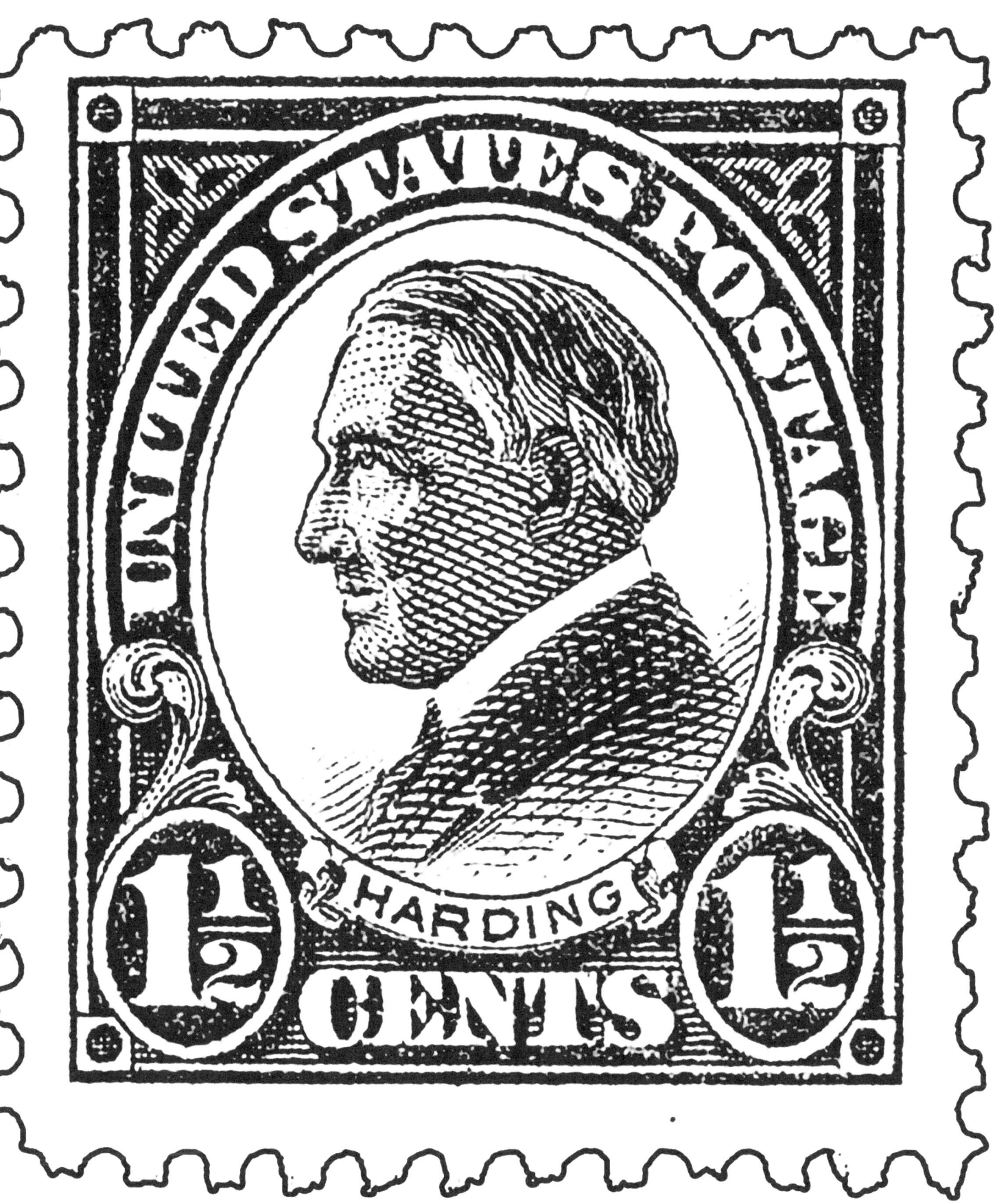

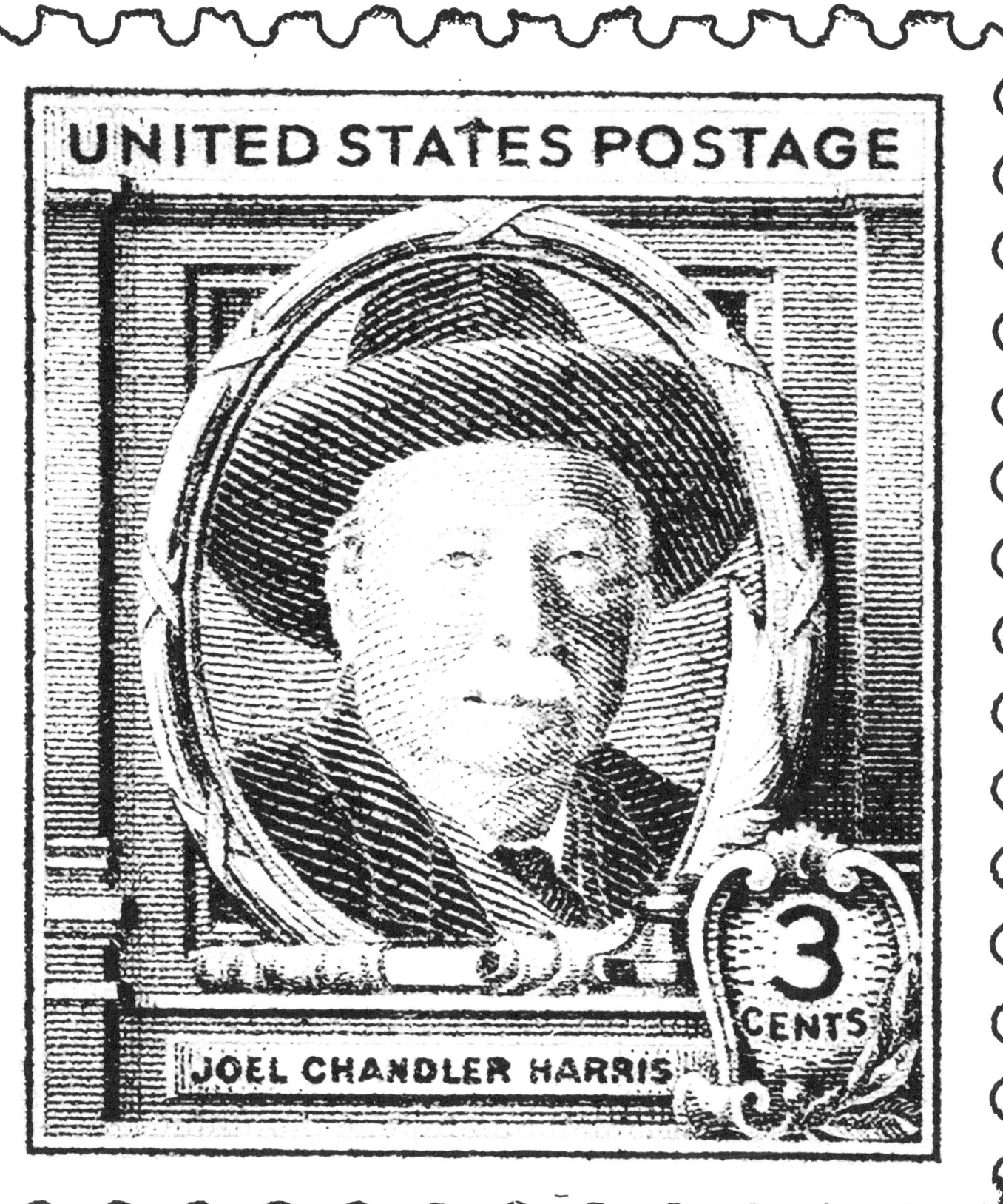

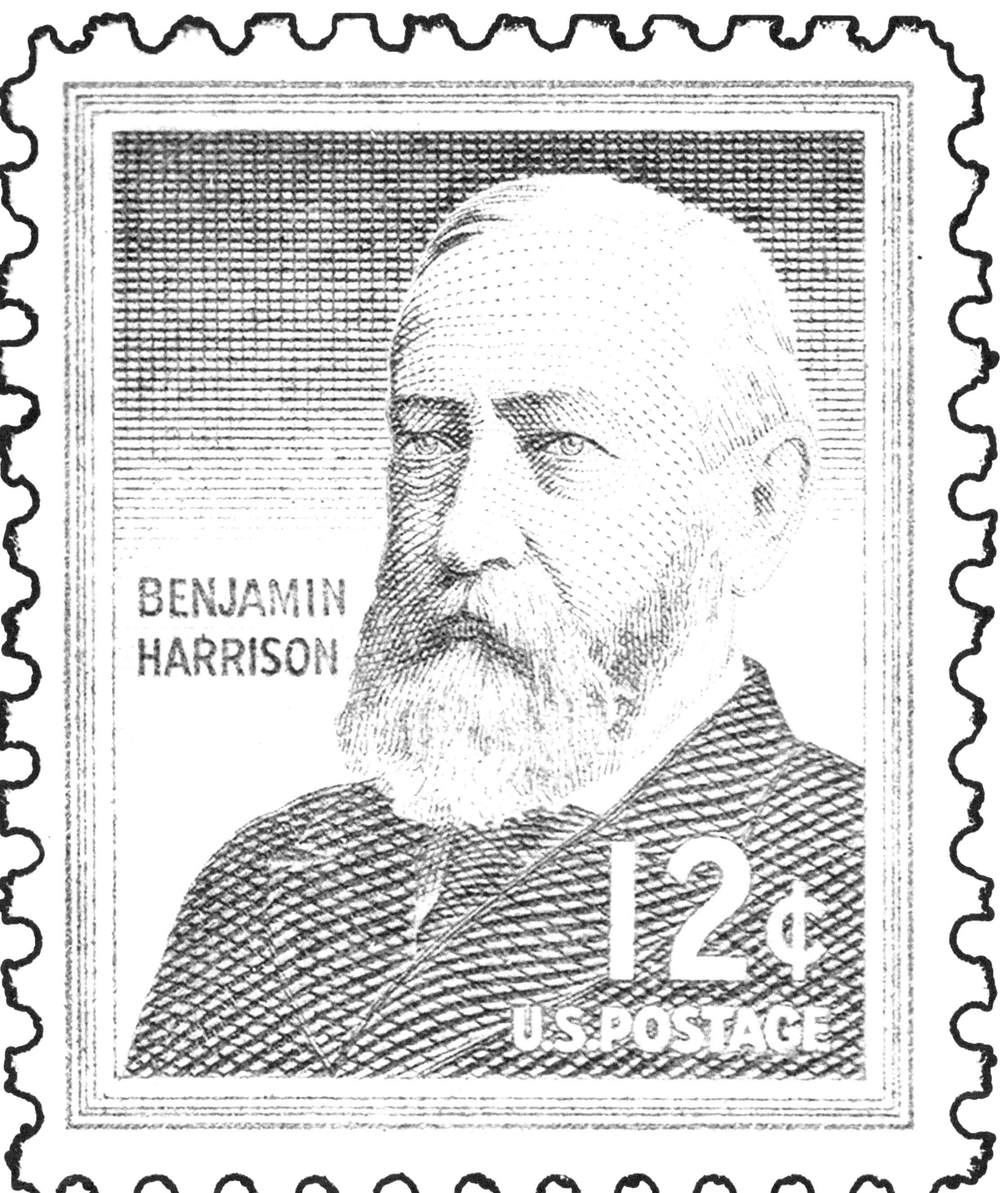

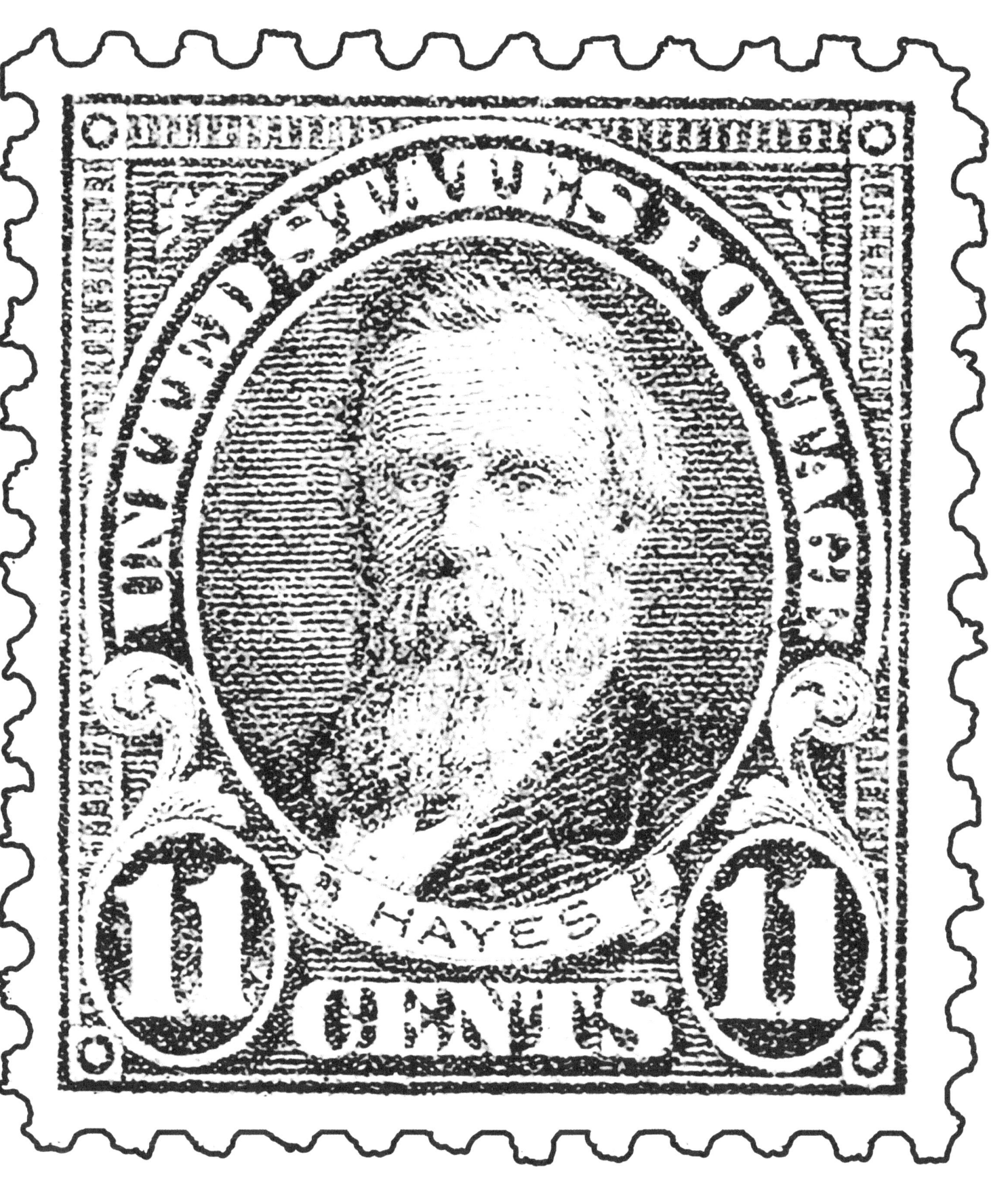

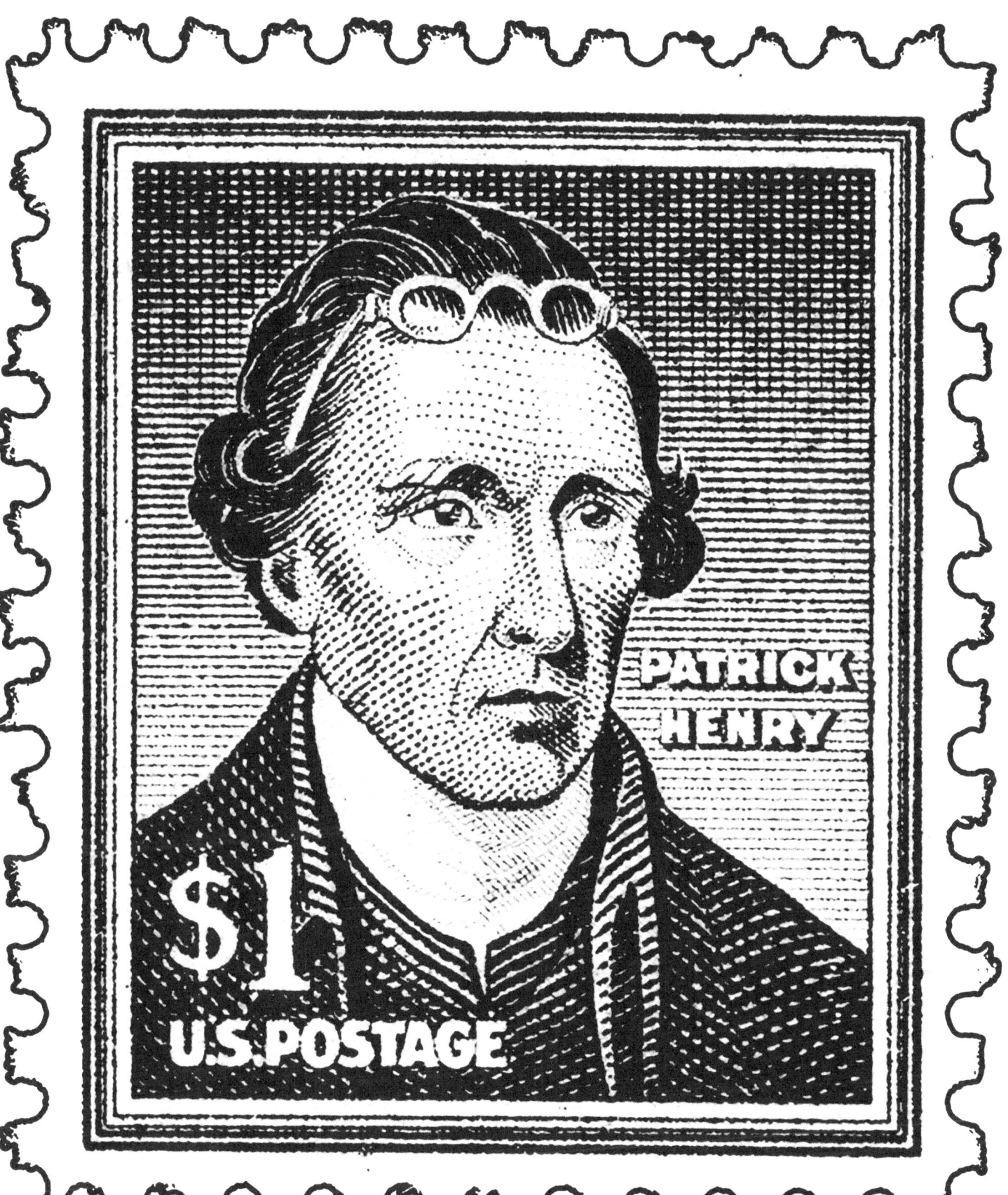

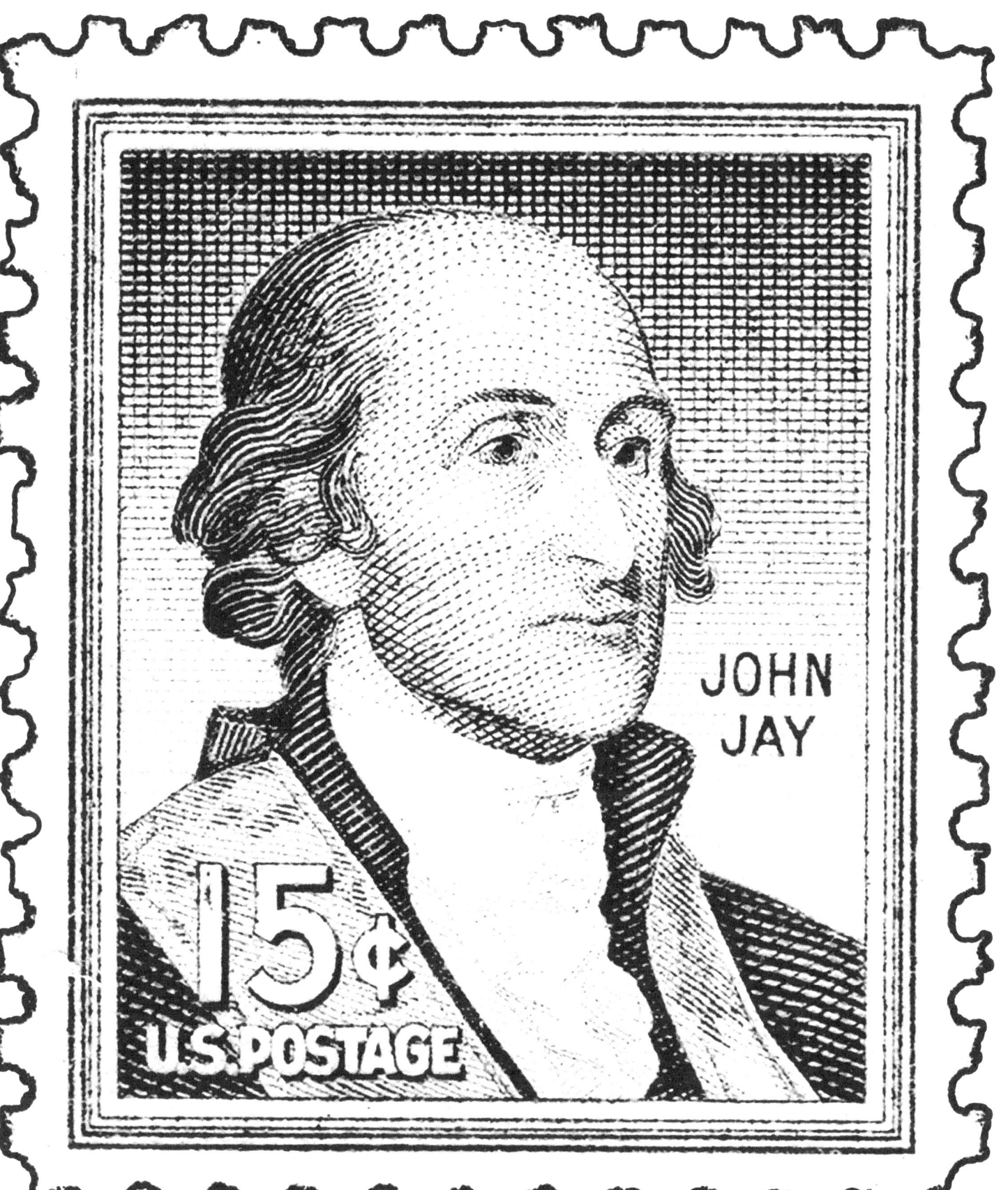

JEFFERSON

2¢ U.S. POSTAGE

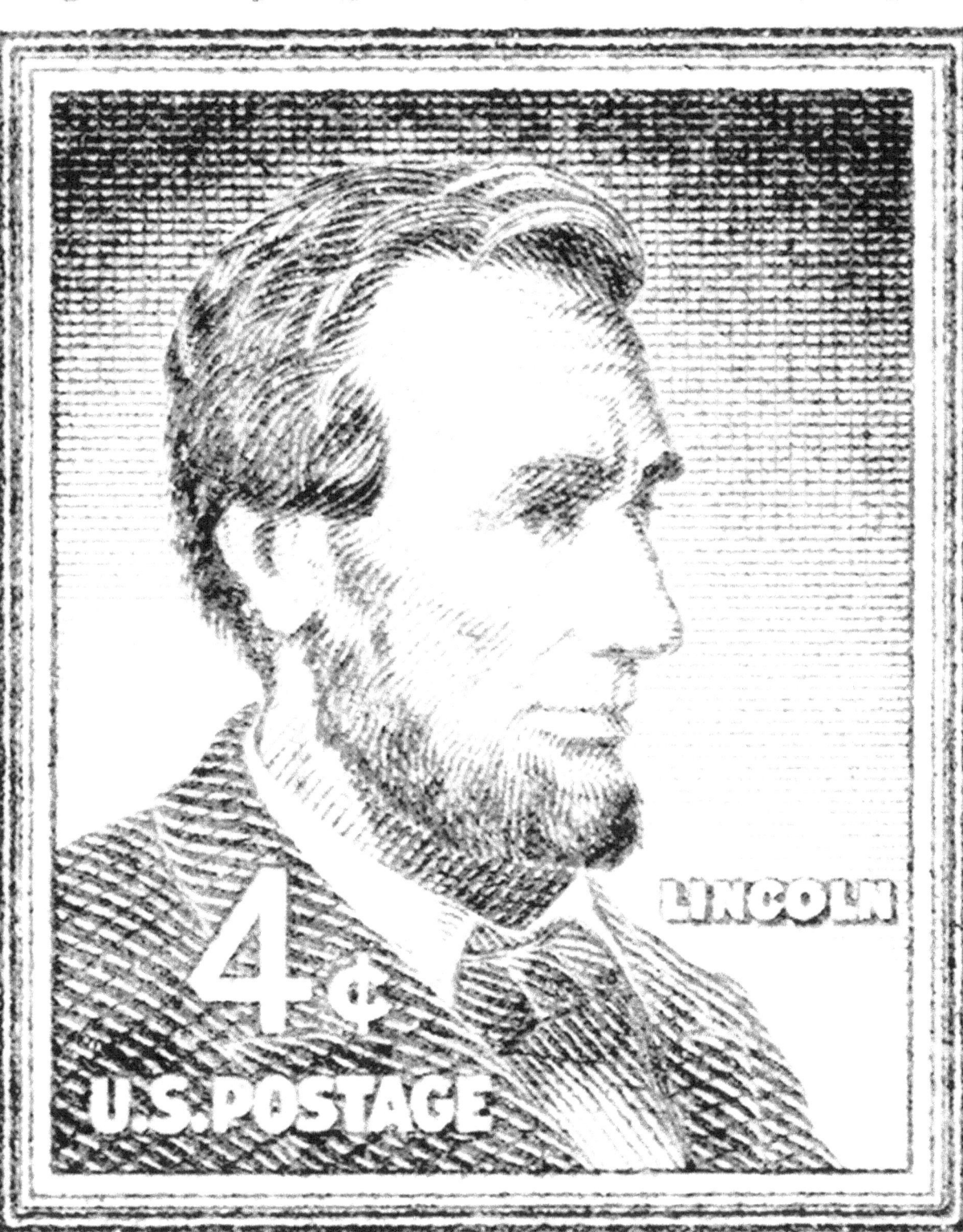

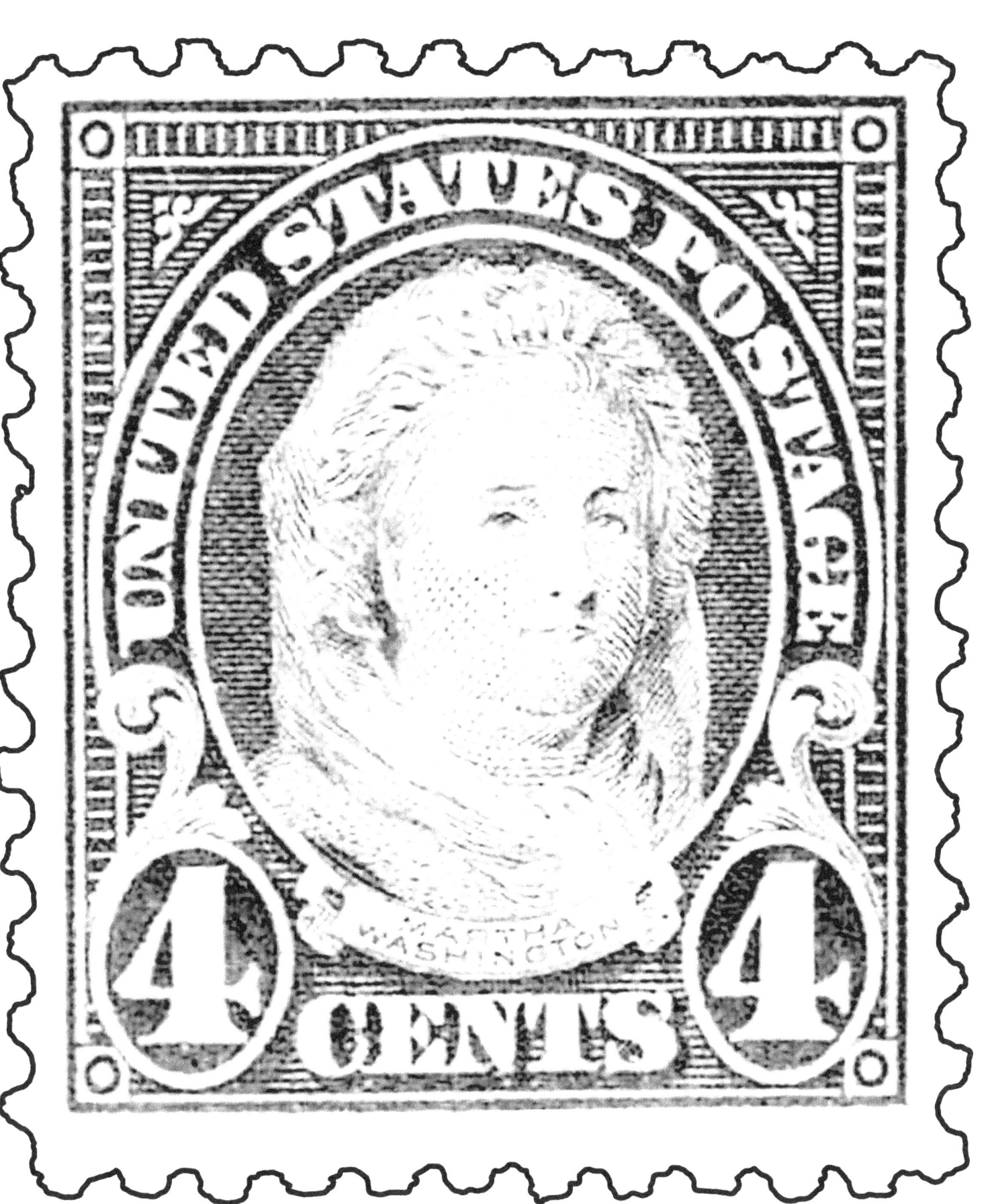

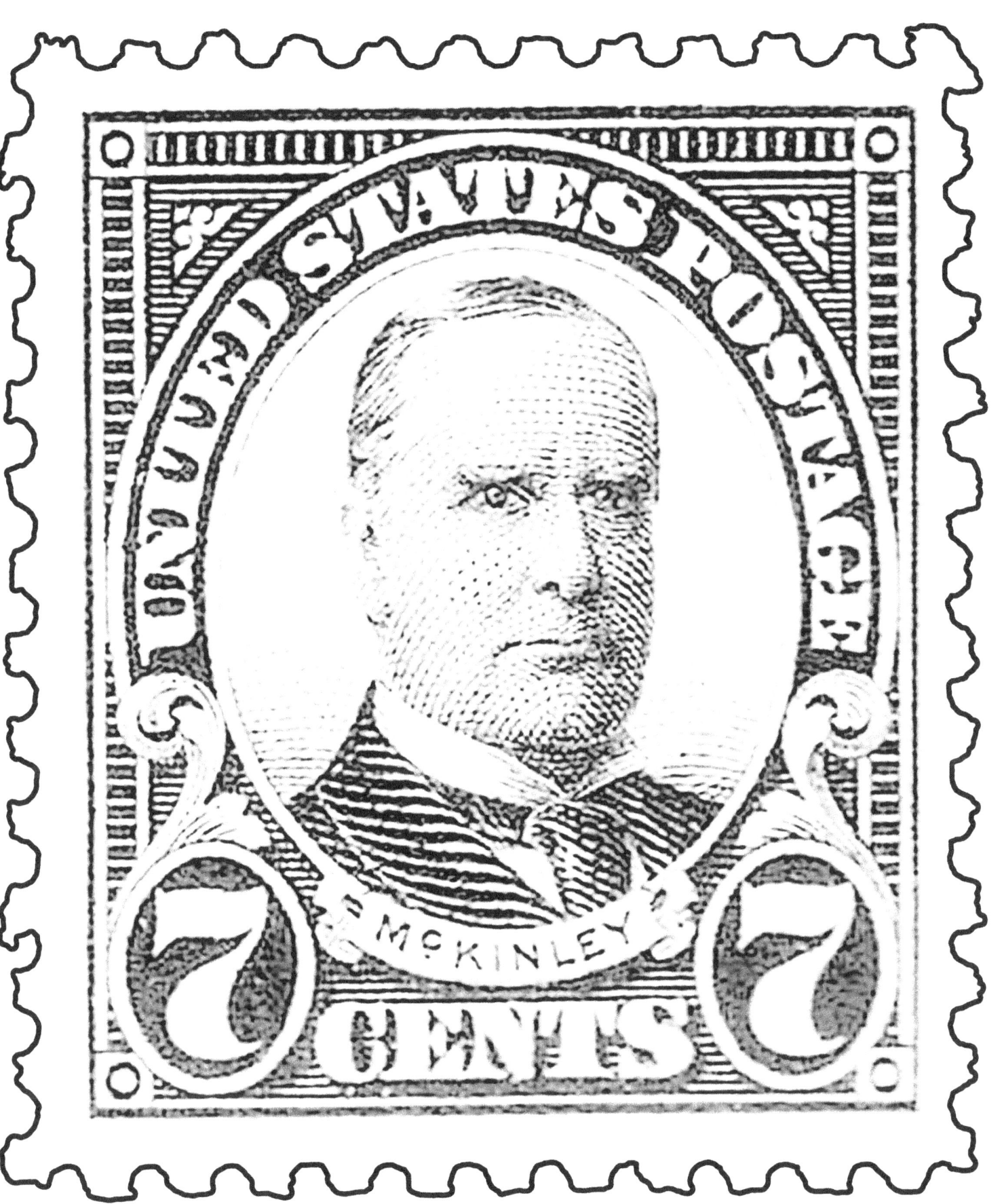

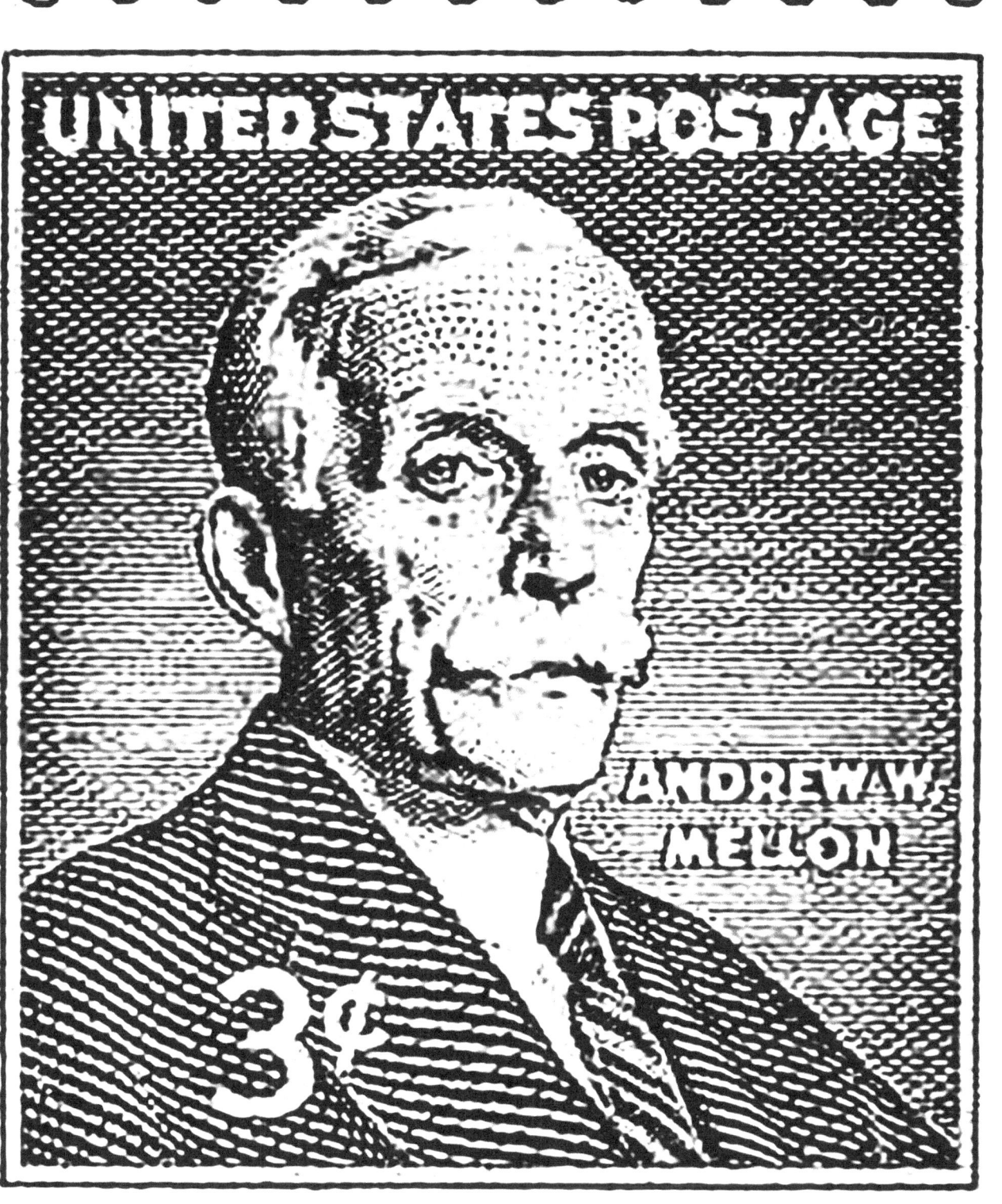

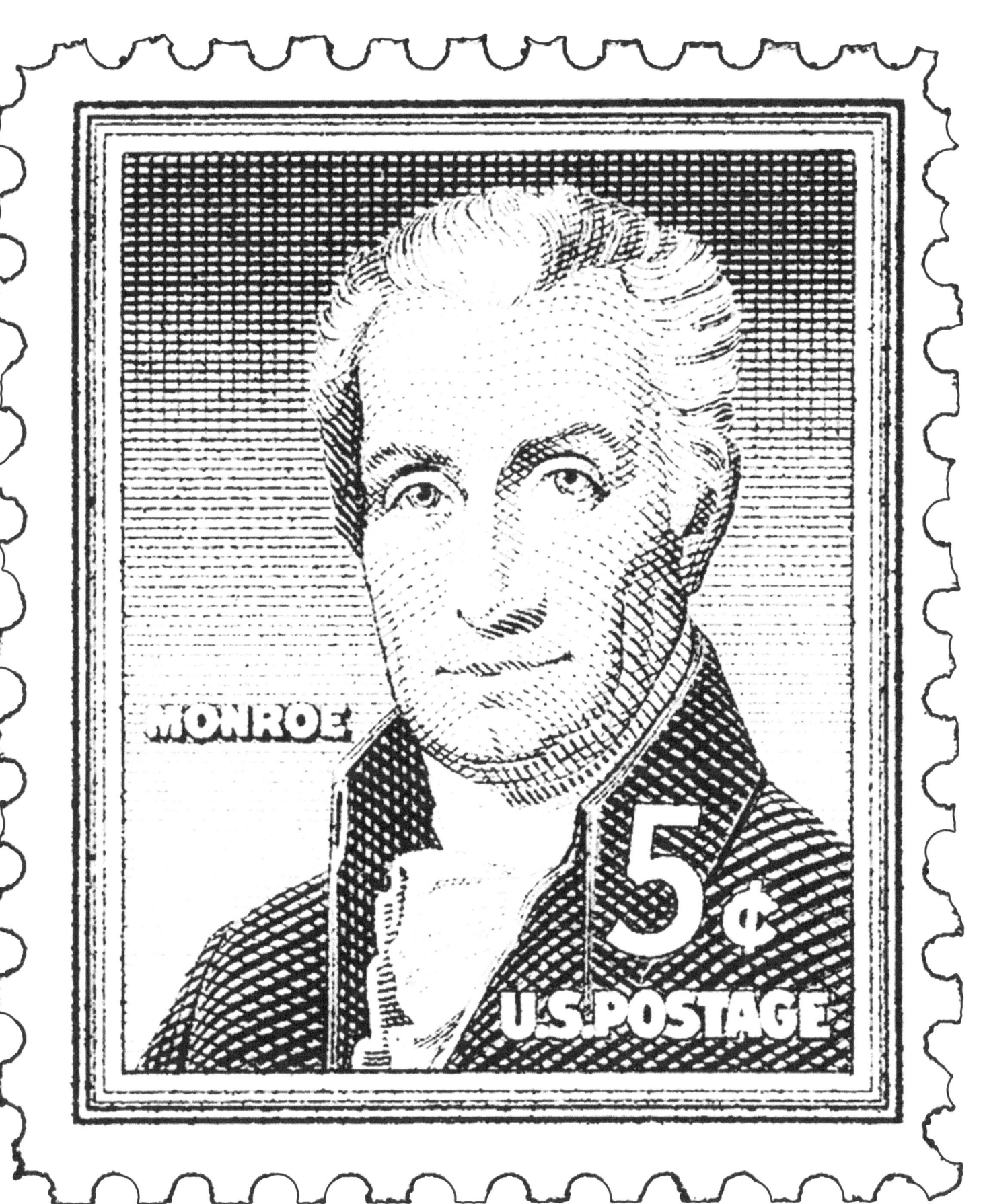

UNITED STATES POSTAGE

1733 — 1933

3 GENERAL OGLETHORPE **3**
CENTS U.S.

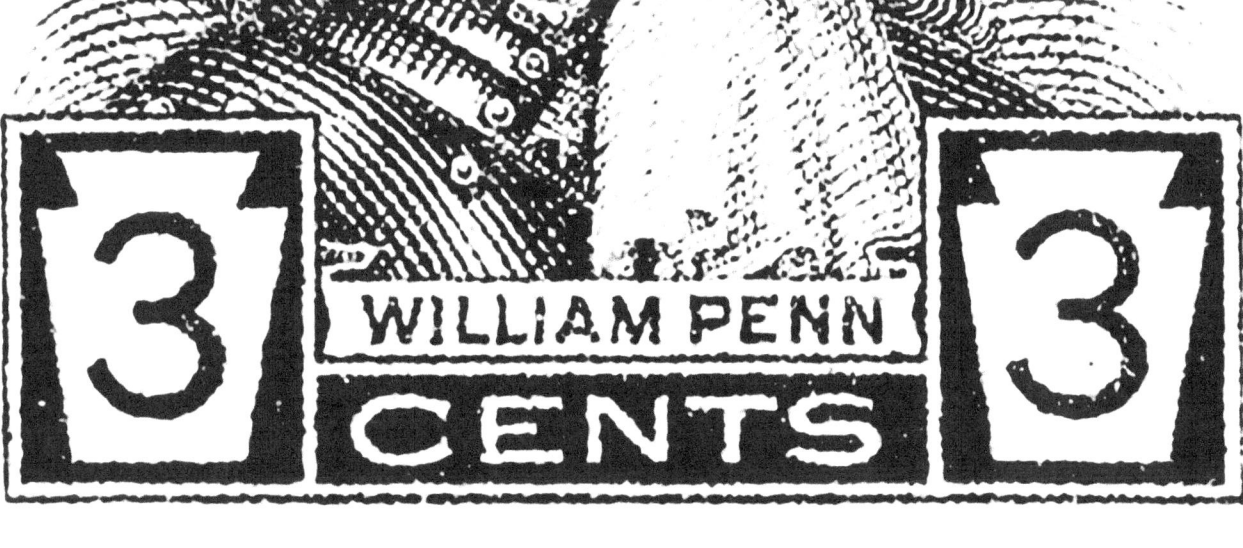

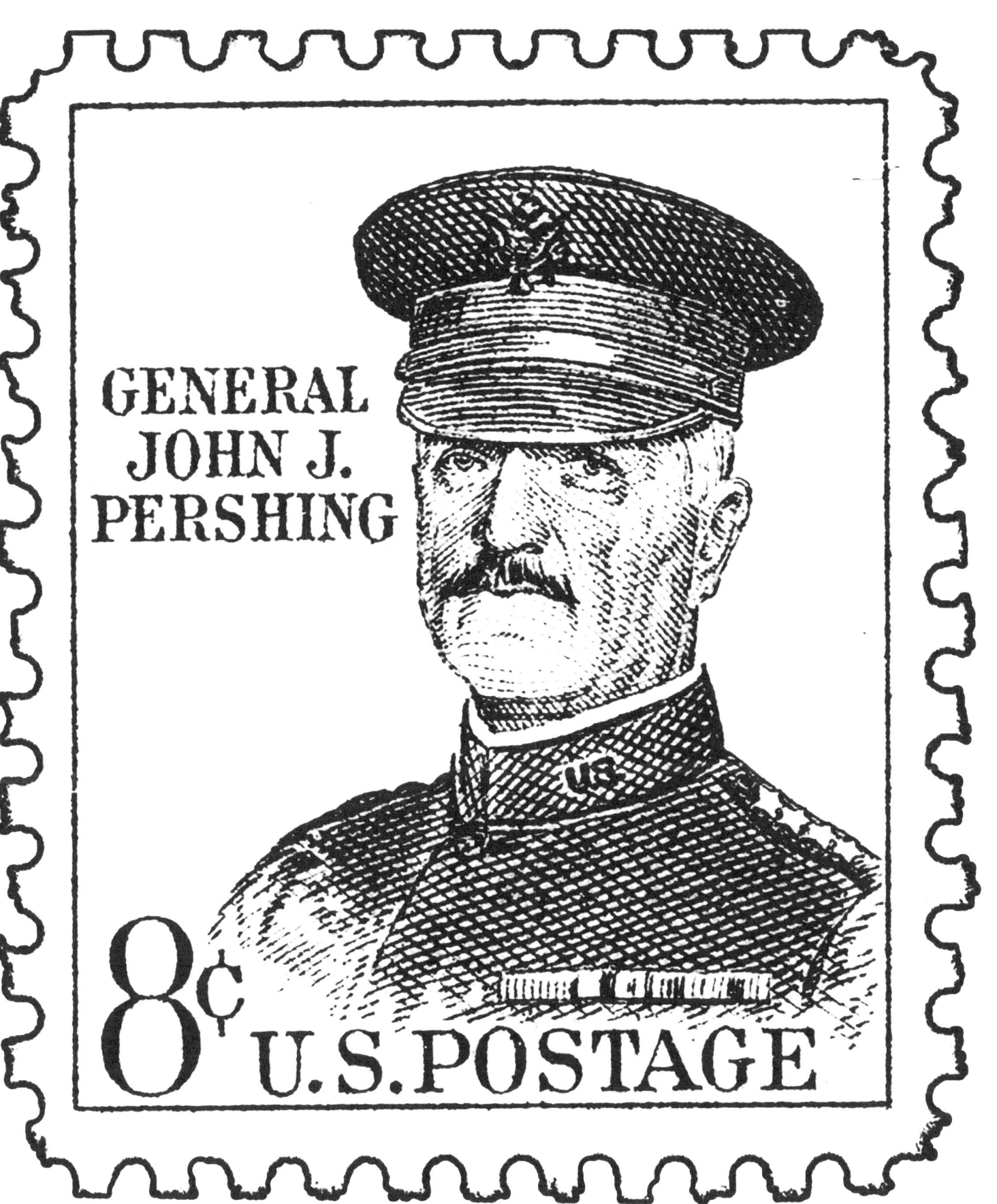

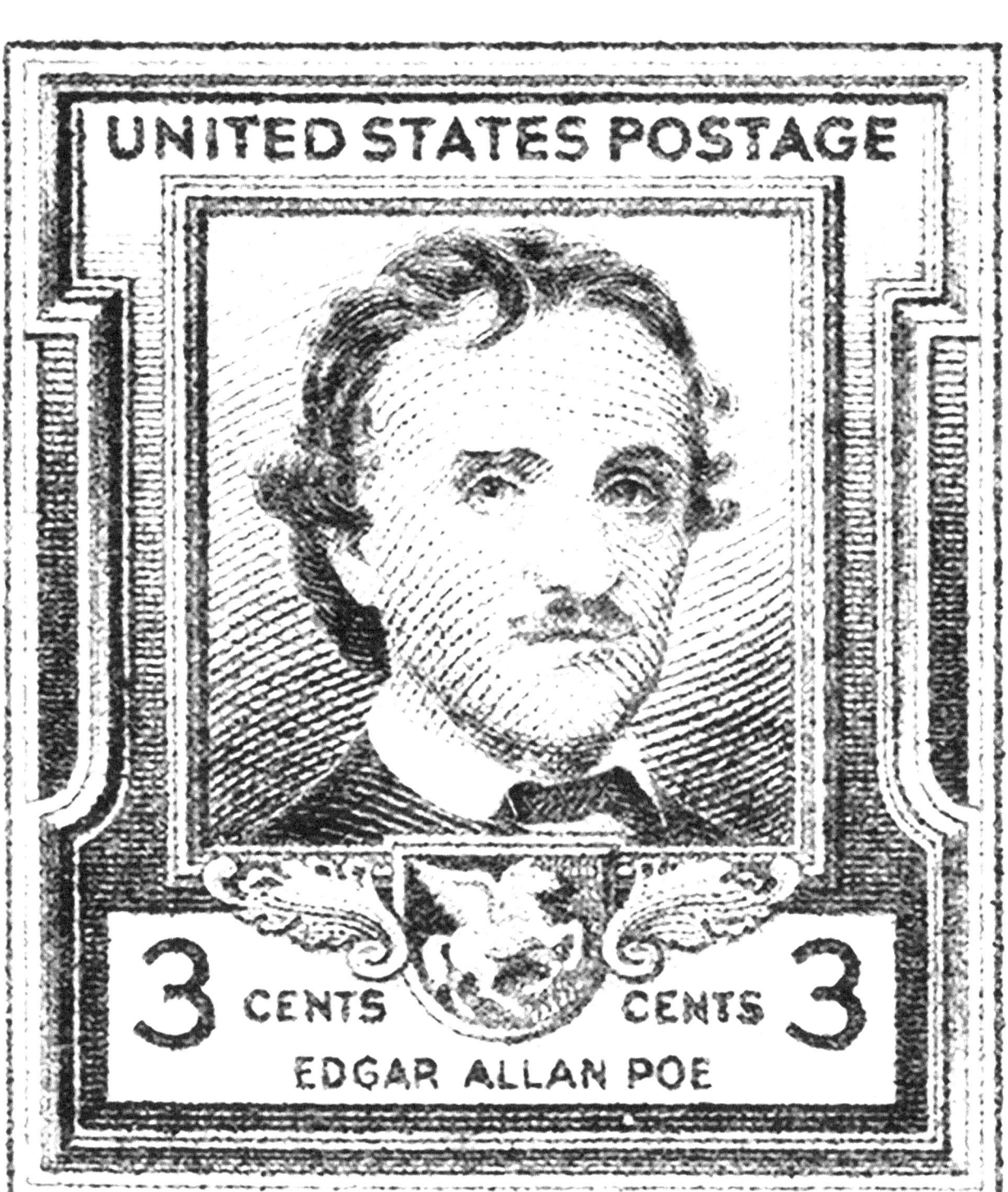

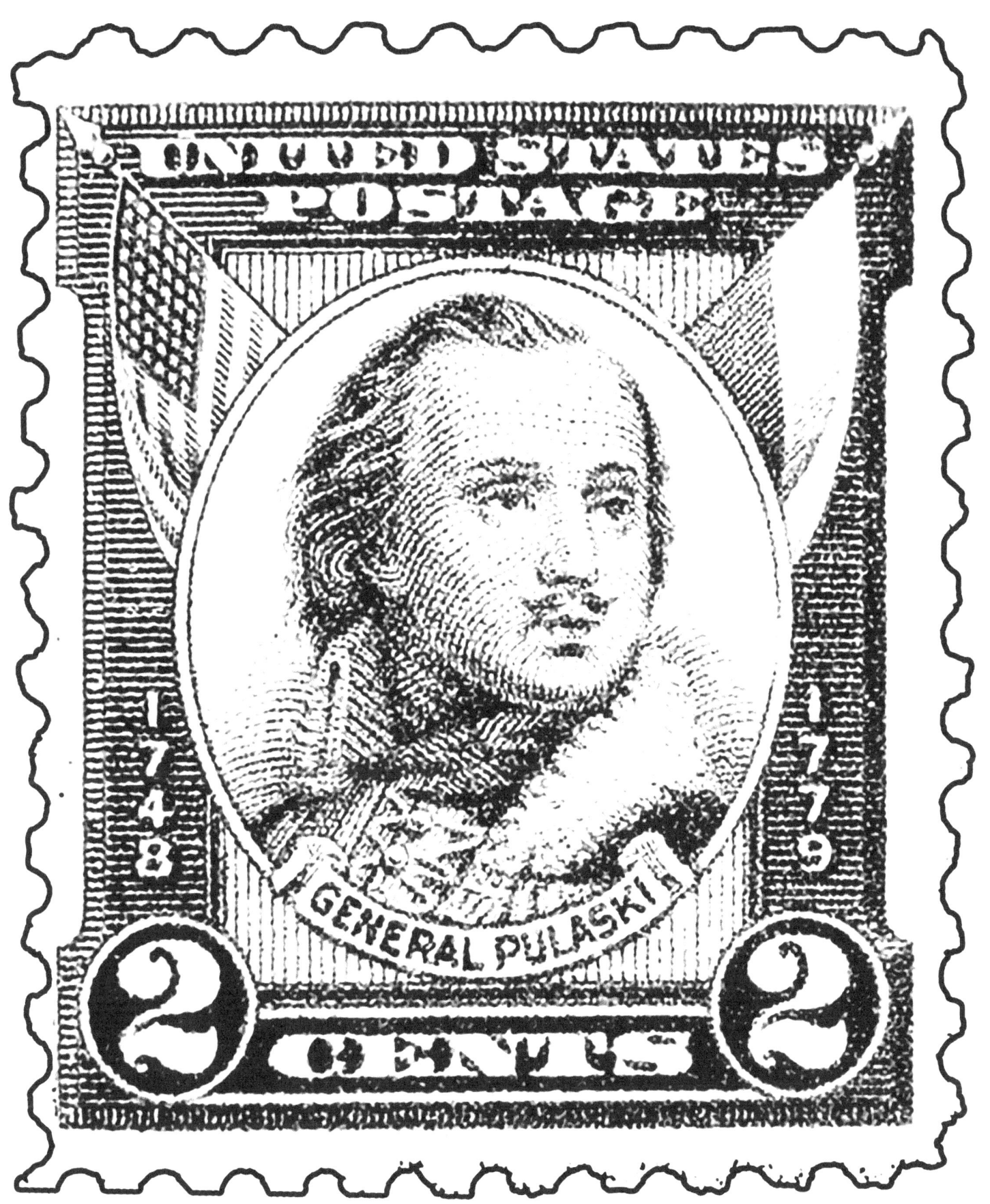

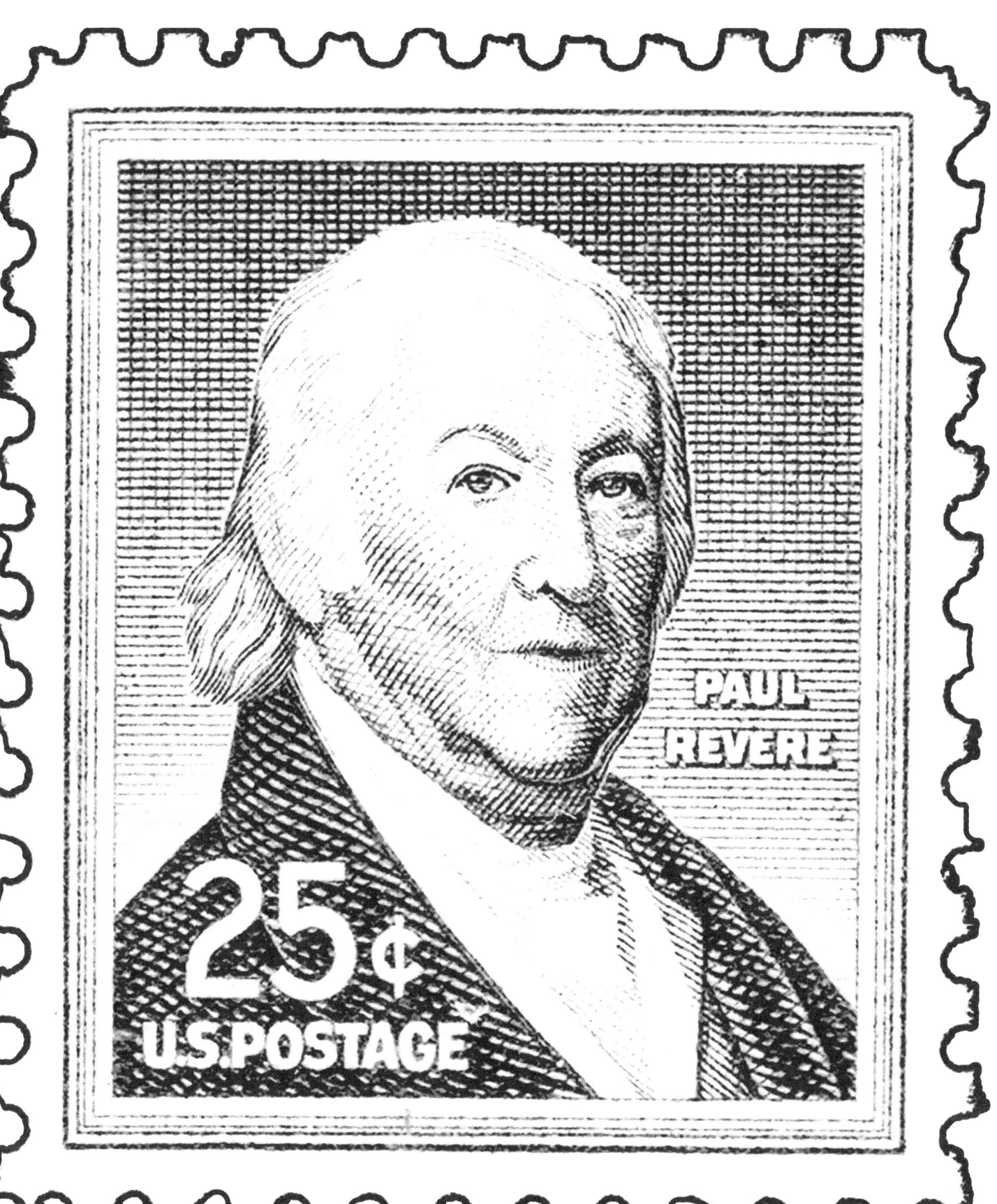

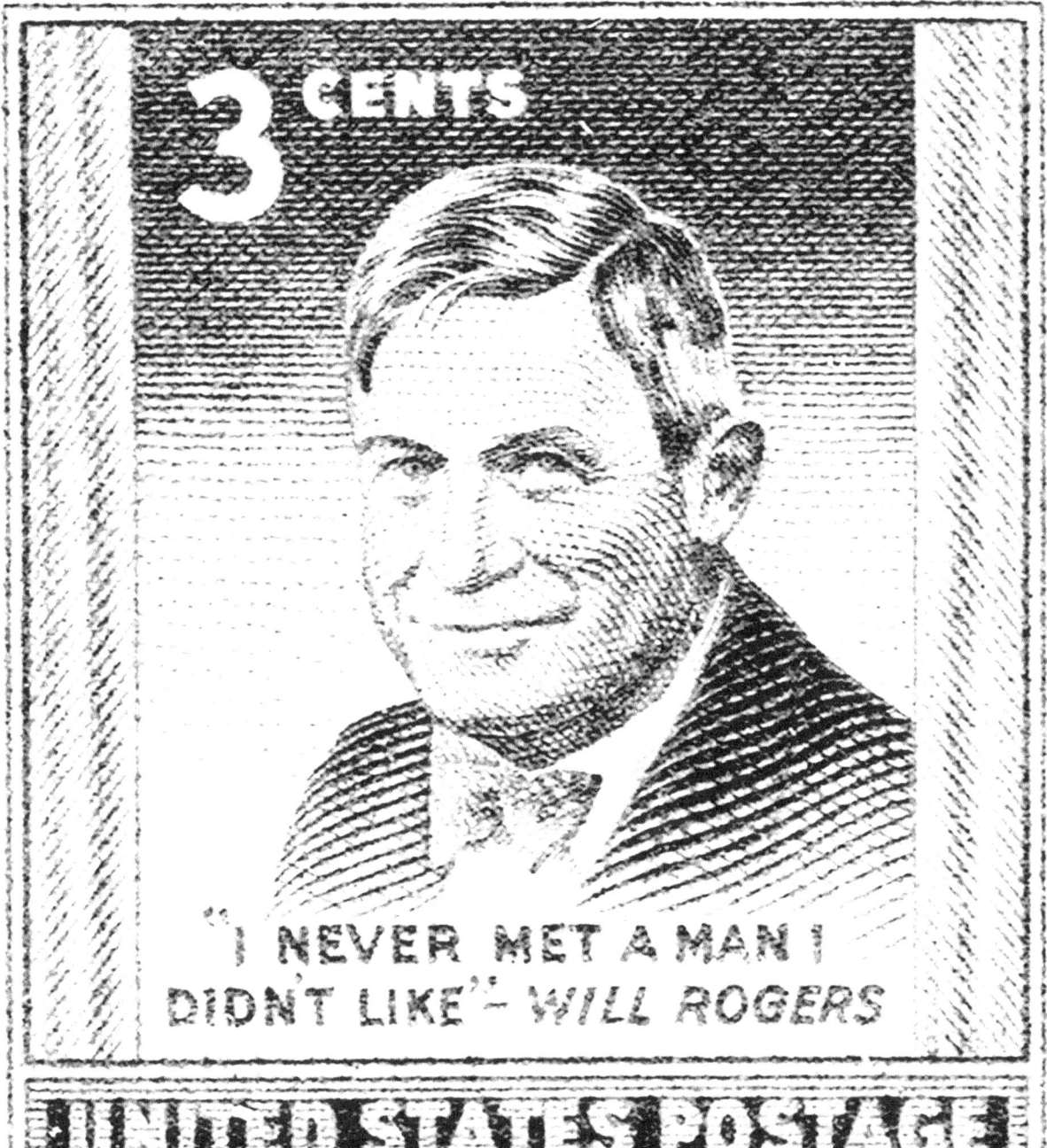

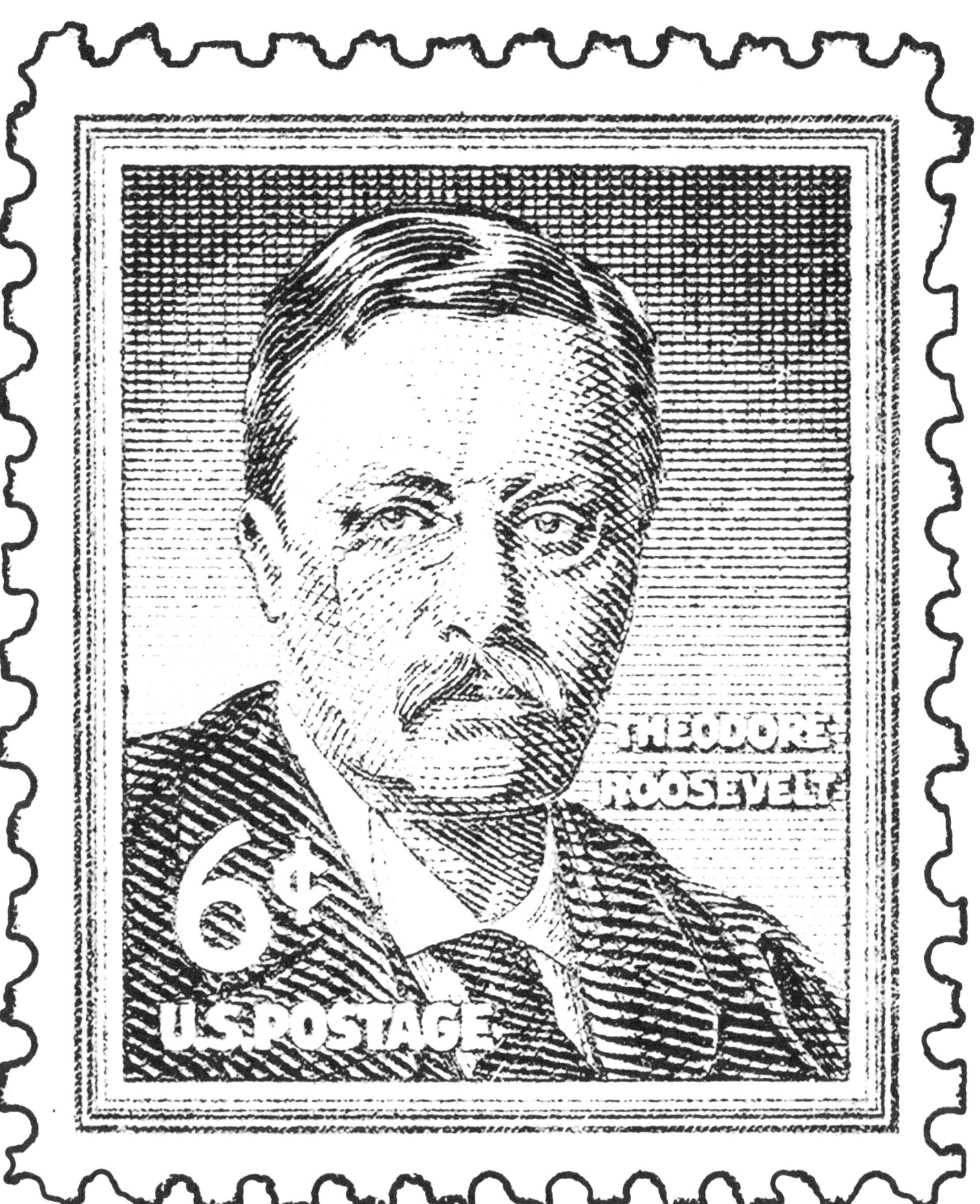

ALFRED E. SMITH

1873
1944

U.S. POSTAGE 3¢

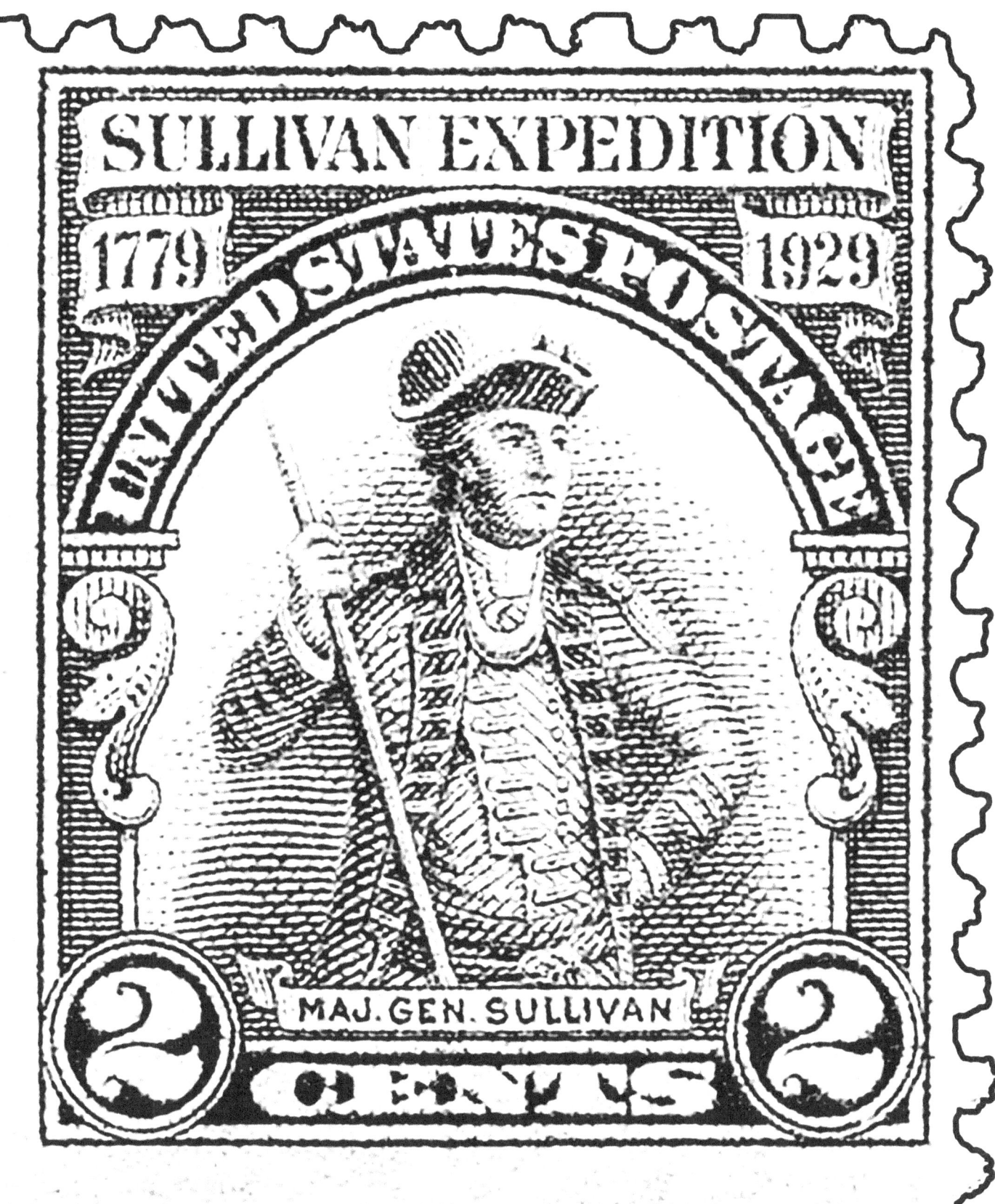

SUSAN B. ANTHONY

50¢

U.S. POSTAGE

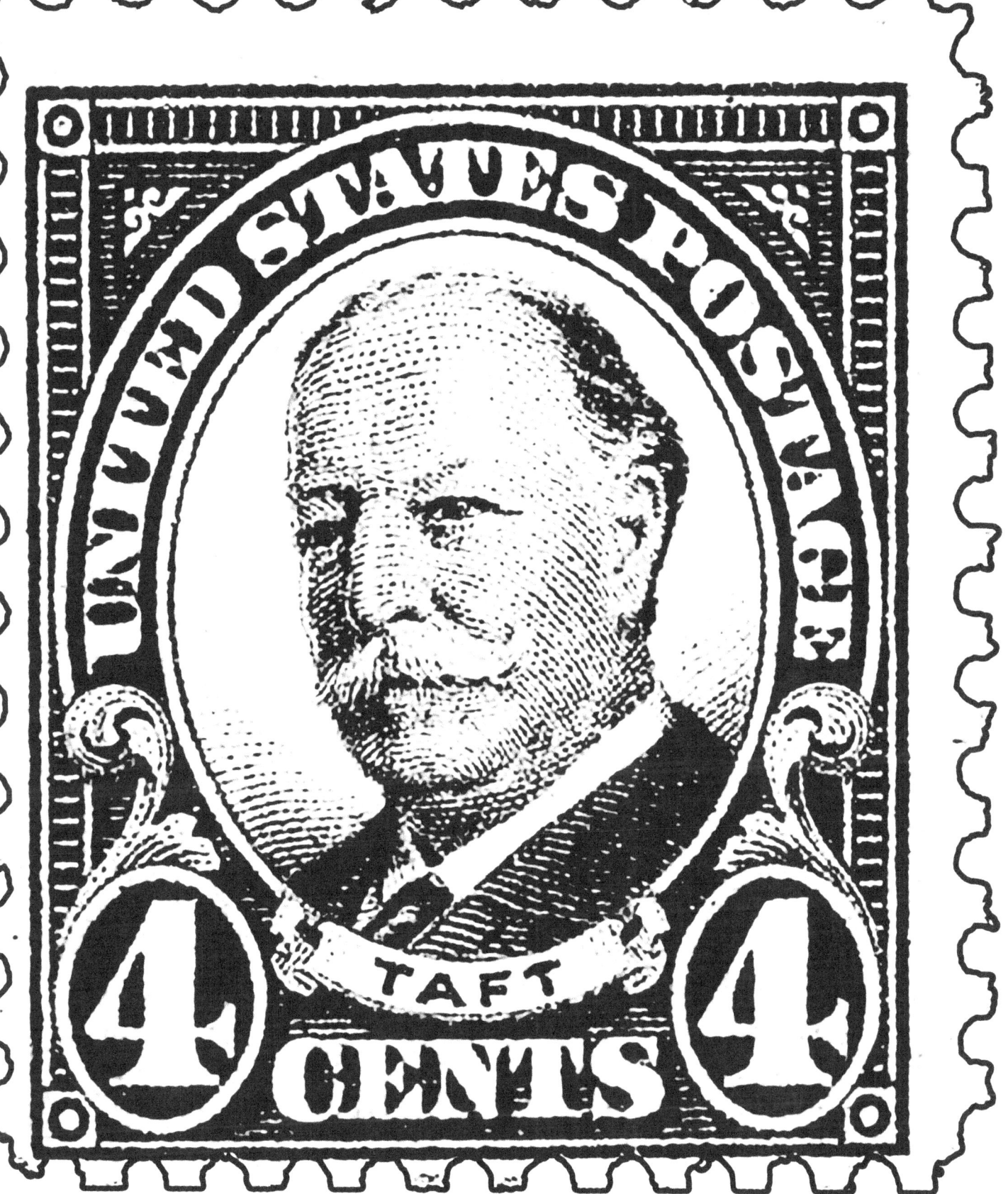

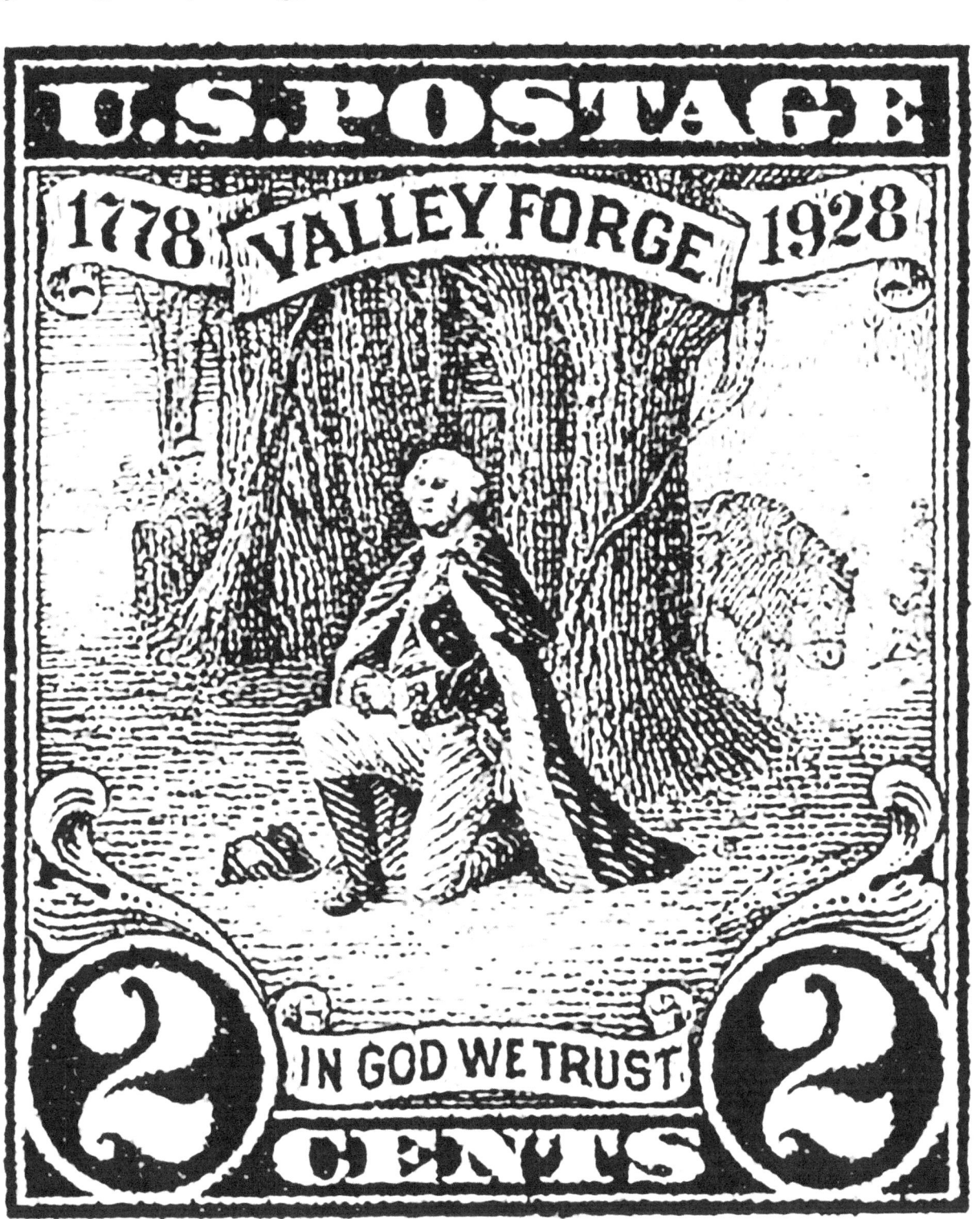

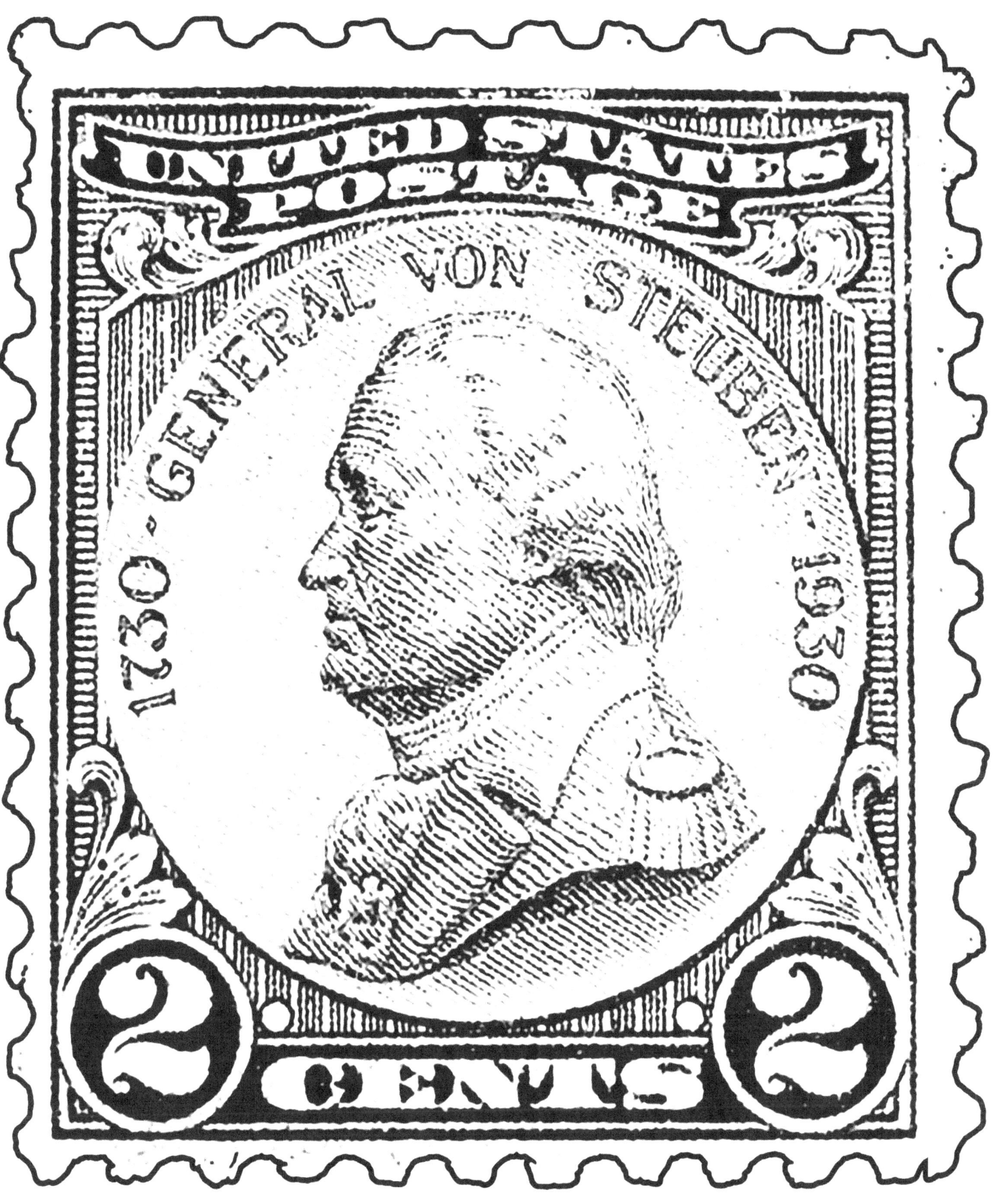

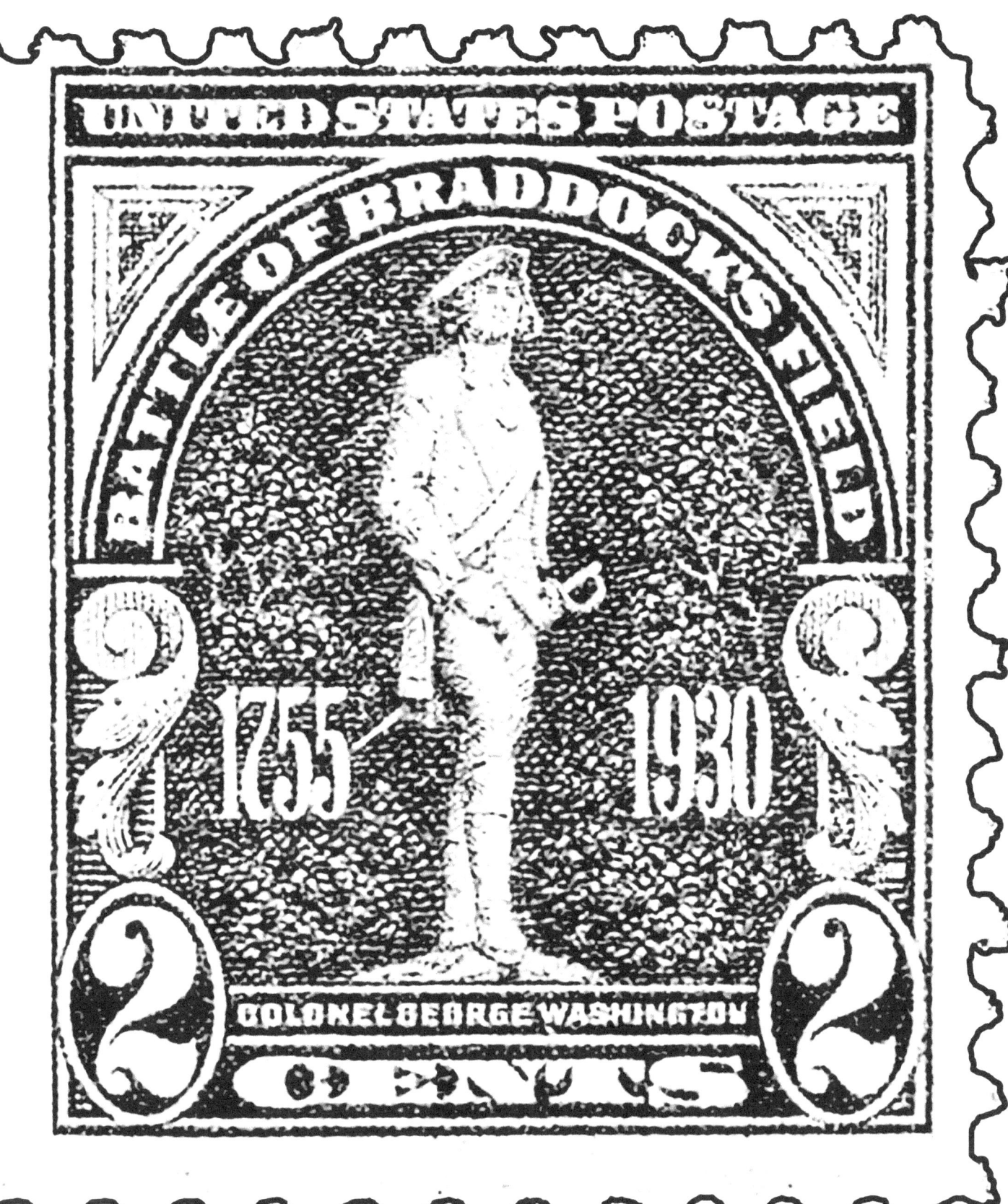

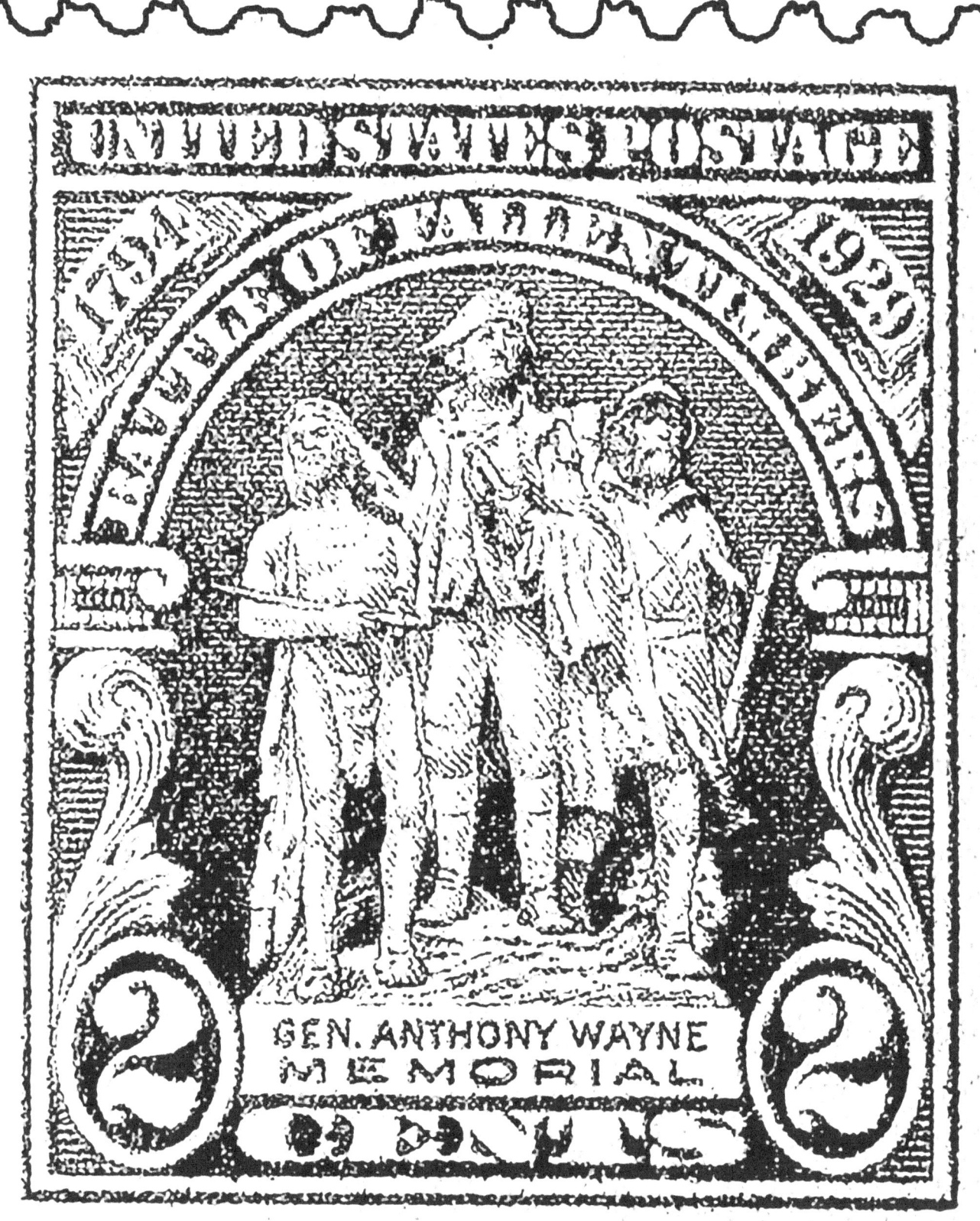

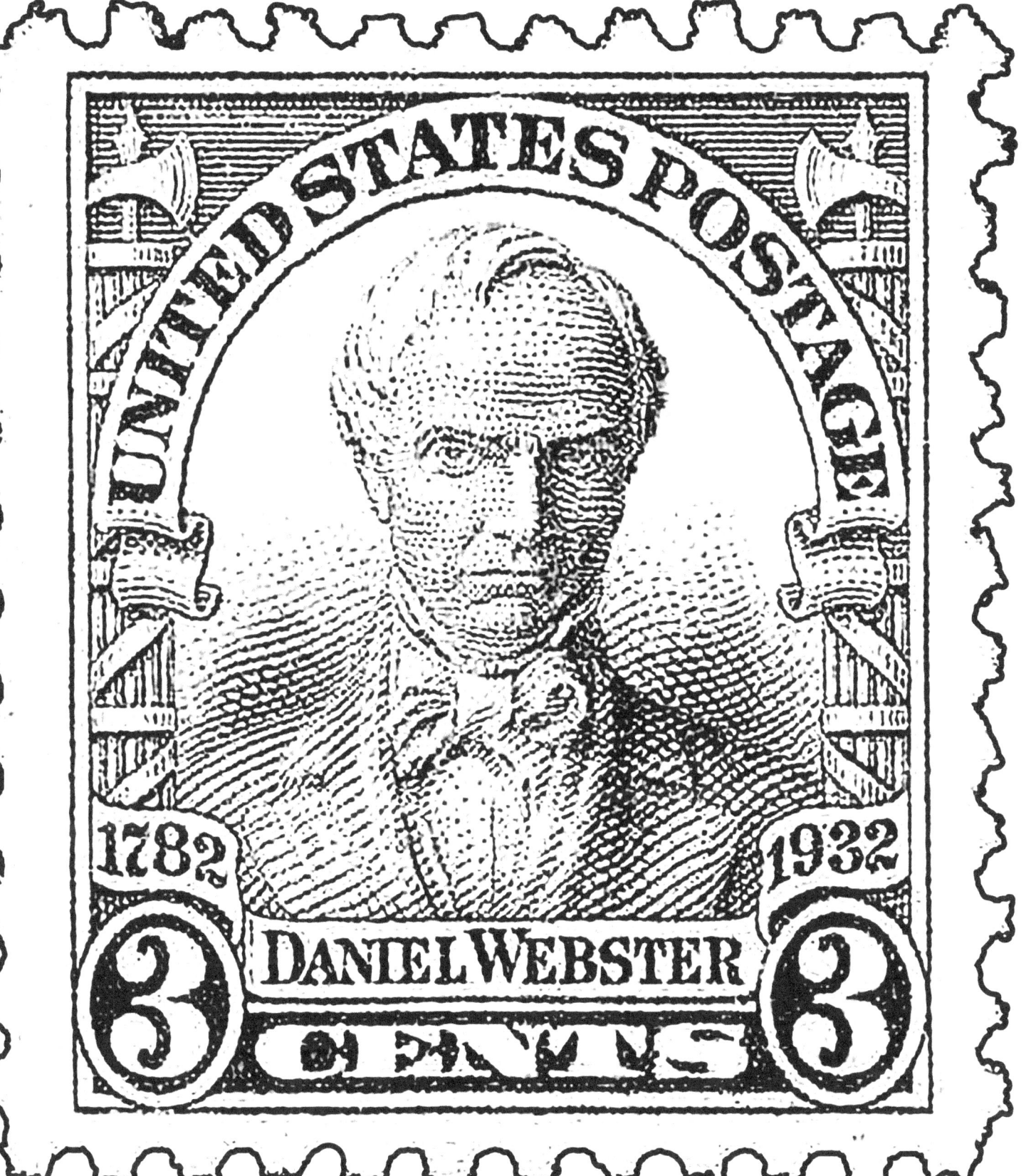

UNITED STATES POSTAGE

WILLIAM ALLEN WHITE

3 CENTS

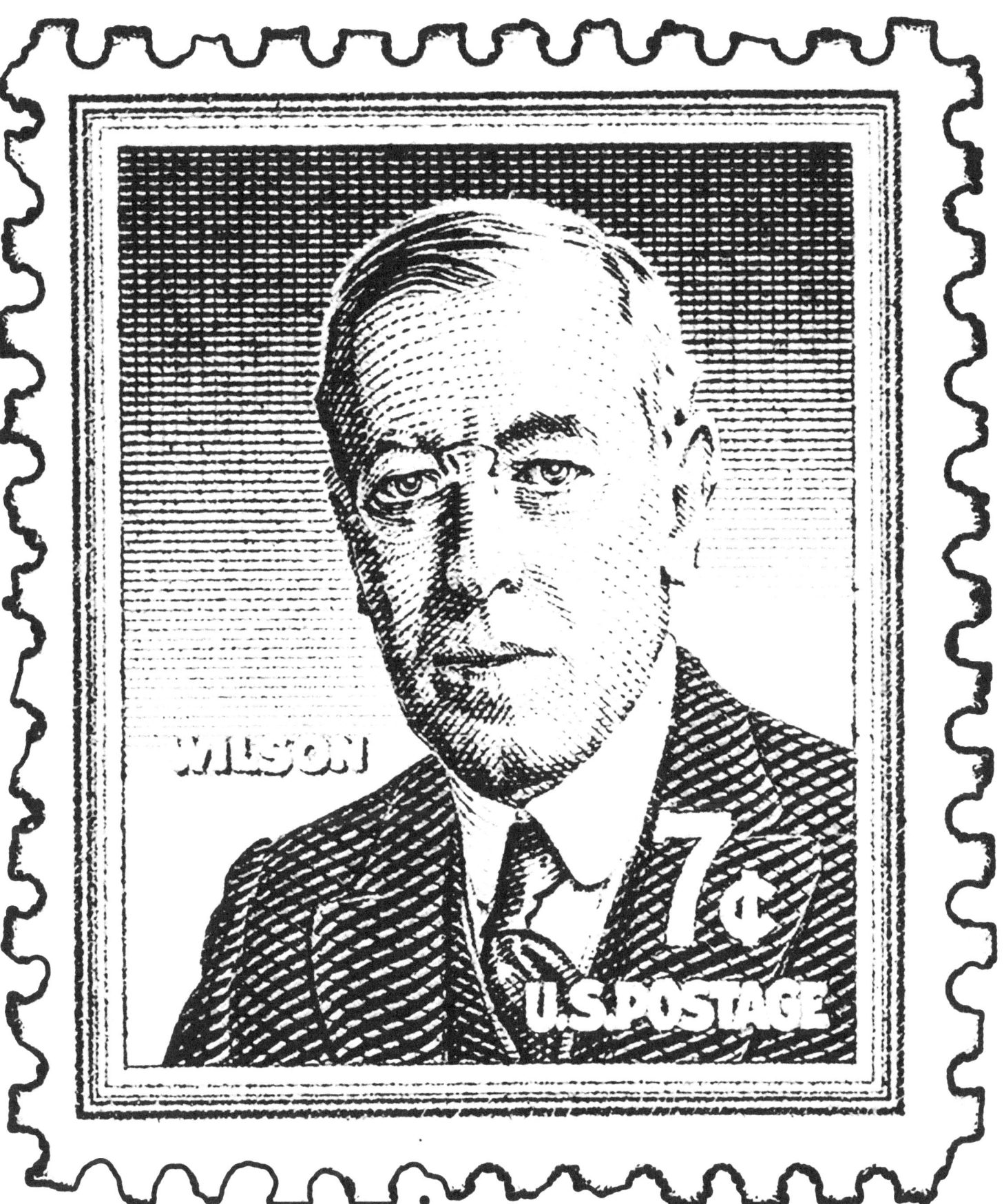